Bending with the Winds

Bending
WITH THE
*Winds*_____
Kurt Waldheim and the United Nations

Seymour Maxwell FINGER
and
Arnold A. SALTZMAN
George Schwab, *Adviser*

New York
Westport, Connecticut
London

For Annette.
 SMF

Library of Congress Cataloging-in-Publication Data

Finger, Seymour Maxwell.
  Bending with the winds : Kurt Waldheim and the United Nations /
Seymour Maxwell Finger and Arnold A. Saltzman.
    p. cm.
  Includes bibliographical references and index.
  ISBN 0-275-93701-1 (lib. bdg. : alk. paper)
  1. United Nations Secretary-General. 2. Waldheim, Kurt.
I. Saltzman, Arnold A. II. Title.
JX1977.A362F53 1990
341.23′24′092—dc20   90-37861

British Library Cataloguing in Publication Data is available.

Library of Congress Catalog Card Number: 90-37861
ISBN: 0-275-93701-1

First published in 1990

Praeger Publishers, One Madison Avenue, New York, NY 10010
An imprint of Greenwood Publishing Group, Inc.

Printed in the United States of America

∞

The paper used in this book complies with the
Permanent Paper Standard issued by the National
Information Standards Organization (Z39.48–1984).

10 9 8 7 6 5 4 3 2 1

Contents

Preface

In 1986 the world was startled by revelations that Kurt Waldheim, former secretary general of the United Nations, had served with German army units in the Balkans in World War II and had been charged with war crimes. These disclosures were more widely disseminated in the United States than in any other country, with the possible exception of Austria. In their treatment of the issue these two countries represented opposite poles. In the United States the media lambasted Waldheim both for his wartime record and for having hidden it. Opponents of the United Nations seized upon the news to discredit the organization itself rather than the major governments, like the United States, which made his election possible. By contrast, the Austrian media were mostly sympathetic to him, citing extenuating circumstances.

Waldheim's subsequent election as president of Austria suggested that these disclosures did not faze the Austrian people. In fact, criticism from abroad aroused a certain chauvinism, seeming to spur the need to defend a fellow Austrian against foreign attacks. The fact that the main instigator of the research that led to the revelations was the World Jewish Congress sparked an anti-Semitism that had never receded far below the surface. This reaction, in turn, evoked memories abroad of the tumultuous welcome

Hitler received when he marched into Vienna to announce Anschluss with his German blood brothers.

As researchers revealed more details about Waldheim's shadowed past, his membership in Nazi organizations and his alleged involvement in war crimes, one central question clamored for answers. How could a man with such a past become secretary general of the United Nations, head of an organization dedicated not only to the maintenance of peace but also to the preservation and advancement of human rights?

This book is the result of our exploration of that question. Our research reveals that the United States, the Soviet Union, Britain, and France all had intelligence files on Waldheim's service in the Balkans with German army units that committed war crimes. Any of these four countries could have vetoed his appointment as secretary general, yet none did, neither in 1971, 1976, nor 1981. Our analysis of the American position is based on a review of more than 200 confidential and secret telegrams exchanged between the U.S. Mission to the United Nations and Washington that we were able to obtain under the Freedom of Information Act. Further, we interviewed the then secretary of state and his top deputies; British, French, and Soviet diplomats who had been involved in the election process; scores of other diplomats, former diplomats, and Secretariat officials; and Waldheim himself—altogether more than one hundred interviews. These provided new insights on how and why Waldheim was elected. They also illuminated the election process itself.

We explored in depth Waldheim's performance as secretary general. Our book first probes the powers and latent powers of that office, as well as its limitations, through a brief historical analysis of the way the five secretaries general—Lie, Hammarskjöld, Thant, Waldheim, and Perez de Cuellar—have carried out their roles. This provides a basis for evaluating Waldheim's performance and the political context in which he performed. We also investigated charges that he was blackmailed by the Soviets, the British, and the Yugoslavs on the basis of their knowledge of his wartime record, but found no evidence of actual blackmail. We did find, however, that in his efforts to please everybody (he was sometimes referred to as ''the headwaiter''), Waldheim yielded readily to pressure from all sides. Much as he had done when the

Nazis took control of Austria, he bent with the prevailing winds of the moment. And he survived. Nevertheless, he did not win the confidence of major political leaders. Except in the case of the Yom Kippur War and the Iran hostage crisis, they tended to regard him and the United Nations of the 1970s as peripheral to their foreign policy objectives.

Now, however, there is a new situation at the United Nations. For almost four decades the Soviets regarded the United Nations as a forum for propaganda, not an organization that should have a meaningful role in keeping the peace. Accordingly, they were quite content with a secretary general like Waldheim, who would not make waves. Under Gorbachev, by contrast, they have strongly advocated a more active, more effective role for the United Nations. And there have already been signs of resurgence, aided by the diplomatic finesse and patient persistence of Secretary General Perez de Cuellar. In 1988–1989, for example, the United Nations negotiated the cease-fire between Iran and Iraq, facilitated the withdrawal of Soviet troops from Afghanistan, and laid the foundation for the peaceful attainment of independence for Namibia (Southwest Africa). If this promising trend endures and the major powers, in cooperation with the other members, continue on their present track of collaboration, the United Nations may at long last carry out the important role in the maintenance of international peace and security envisaged in its charter. And there are urgent new challenges not foreseen when that charter was written—threats to the environment that cry out for international cooperation, the dangers implicit in the international drug traffic, the continuing menace of international terrorism, the critical needs of more than 17 million refugees and the shame of widespread hunger in a world capable of producing enough food for all. Altogether, these challenges and opportunities constitute a crucial agenda for the future.

These considerations led us to our third quest, the search for a procedure that will produce the kind of leadership required for a revitalized United Nations. This means a secretary general with outstanding qualities of integrity, intelligence, courage, creativity, and leadership. It means the kind of thorough search that would have prevented the election of a Waldheim. The job is much too important to be left to chance. It is linked to the future of humanity.

Acknowledgments

The idea for this volume was first proposed by my co-author, Arnold Saltzman. I am very thankful to him for this conception and for his many helpful suggestions as the work progressed.

A significant part of the drafting was done at the Villa Serbelloni, the Rockefeller Foundation retreat for scholars on Lake Como. One could not have asked for an environment more conducive to productive work. The setting was magnificent. The villa staff was remarkably supportive, quietly and efficiently taking care of every need. The colleagues were a very special group who made a permanent impact on me. I am most grateful to the foundation for providing this memorable experience.

Much of the work on the United Nations was done at the Ralph Bunche Institute of the City University of New York, where I am now a senior fellow. I am particularly grateful to Dr. Benjamin Rivlin, director of the institute, for his encouragement, and to Nancy Okada, its administrator, and Annette Phillips for their patient, competent, and careful assistance in typing and proofreading the manuscript.

Valuable research aid was provided by Liesl G. Lissauer and Vivienne S. Manber of the Reference Section of the U.S. Mission to the United Nations. Over 200 confidential and secret telegrams were declassified and made available by the Information and

Privacy Staff of the United States Department of State, and I am most grateful to them.

I am also indebted to the scores of present and former American officials, foreign diplomats and U.N. Secretariat officials who kindly agreed to be interviewed. They are too numerous to be acknowledged individually, but many of their names appear in the "Among Those Interviewed" section in the notes for chapter 1.

My thanks go also to Dr. Robert Edwin Herzstein and to William Morrow and Co., Inc., for granting permission to quote from Dr. Herzstein's book, *Waldheim: The Missing Years*; I owe special thanks to Dr. Giuseppe Ammendola, who is largely responsible for the index.

Most of all I want to thank my wife, Annette. She provided not only the love and encouragement of a most devoted companion but also the patience and critical judgment I needed at every step.

Seymour Maxwell Finger

This will acknowledge with appreciation the willingness of former Secretary of State William P. Rogers, to discuss Waldheim with me.

I would also like to express my gratitude to Ambassador Seymour Maxwell Finger for being as knowledgable and pleasant a collaborator as one could hope to find.

Arnold A. Saltzman

Chapter 1

Who Is Kurt Waldheim?

He is the grandson of a Moravian blacksmith who moved to Austria. His father was a teacher and school administrator in rural Austria. He became secretary general of the United Nations in 1971 and was reelected for five more years in 1976. In 1986 he became president of Austria. This is the "success story" of Kurt Waldheim.

Yet even as he campaigned for the presidency in 1986, the dark side of Waldheim's career emerged. An article planted by his political opponents in the Viennese journal, *Profil,* on 9 March 1986 revealed that Waldheim had served as an intelligence officer with Germany army units that were involved in war crimes in Yugoslavia and Greece consisting of the murder of Yogoslavian civilians, the execution of captured British commandos, and the deportation of Jews to concentration camps. In his memoirs Waldheim carefully avoided any mention of his wartime service in the Balkans, and has repeatedly lied about it to his closest co-workers in the U.N. Secretariat.[1] These revelations triggered an investigation by the World Jewish Congress that unearthed evidence of his involvement in Yugoslavia and Greece and charges of war crimes filed by Yugoslavia with the U.N. War Crimes Commission in 1948.[2] Nevertheless, following these revelations and the extensive publicity about them in Austria and abroad, Waldheim won the election for president.

What kind of man is Kurt Waldheim? What were his beliefs, his interests, his background, and his path toward high positions? Above all, how was he elected secretary general of the United Nations? Why did the major governments with veto power in the United Nations support his election? How much did they know about his wartime record? Why were the United States, the Soviet Union, Britain, and France prepared to reelect him in 1976 and again in 1981? These are questions that have titillated and troubled people throughout the world as the revelations of the dark side of Waldheim proliferated. We will delve into these unanswered riddles rather than explore extensively into his wartime activities. These are fully described and documented in books by Robert Edwin Herzstein and by Bernard Cohen and Luc Rosenzweig.[3]

Kurt's father, Walter, was one of eleven children born to a Moravian blacksmith named Watzlawik who had moved to the small village of St. Andra-Wordern near Vienna. Walter became the local schoolmaster and married one of the three daughters of the mayor. He was a staunch Catholic and supporter of the Habsburg monarchy until it fell in 1918. Shortly before Kurt's birth in 1918 Walter Watzlawik changed the family name to the Teutonic-sounding Waldheim. The father's career as a teacher and school administrator advanced steadily during the 1920s, and he became superintendent of schools for the district of Tulln.

There was no secondary school in his home village, and Kurt had to travel twenty kilometers to the Gymnasium in Klosterneuberg, rising at five o'clock in the morning. He attributes some of his stamina to this and rigors of his youth, described in a chapter of his book, *In the Eye of the Storm*, entitled "Survivor Course."[4] Kurt also gives much credit to his father, who "regarded nothing as more important than the proper education of his three children and willingly did without to meet our school expenses." Kurt's brother, Walter, who died in 1974, followed in his father's footsteps, pursuing a teaching career. Their sister Linde, became Chief of Radiology at a clinic in Vienna.

Waldheim, while paying tribute to his father, does not write about his mother. But his daughter, Lieselotte, described her paternal grandmother as a loving, courageous woman who took care of the family's physical needs and kept up their morale even during the most difficult wartime years. She also saw to it that

the family came together frequently and kept up intrafamily relationships.[5] Lieselotte noted that her paternal grandfather, Walter Waldheim, did a great deal of painting as a hobby. A number of very creditable still lifes signed by him were on the walls of her home.

After the fall of the Habsburg monarchy in 1918, Walter Waldheim became active in the Christian Social party, a conservative Catholic group. He was an avowed supporter of Austria's independence and both anti-Nazi and anti-Anschluss with Germany. He attended public meetings, at which he was often the speaker, and enjoyed considerable status in the district because of his involvement in community affairs.

The Christian Social party and its leader in 1938, Kurt von Schuschnigg, opposed the Nazi takeover of Austria, and the Waldheims, including Kurt, actively campaigned for him in the 1938 referendum on Austrian independence. As a result their home was defaced by Nazi vandals and young Kurt was beaten up by a gang of Nazi hoodlums.

After the Anschluss, Walter Waldheim was interrogated by the Gestapo and arrested. Although he was quickly released, he lost his job as school superintendent, and his pension was cut. Moreover, Kurt's scholarship to the Consular Academy was cancelled, imposing an additional financial burden on the family. Kurt had to borrow money from relatives and tutor in Latin and Greek.

At this point Kurt apparently decided to go along in order to get along. He was enrolled in the National Socialist Students League on 1 April 1938. Later that year he became a member of the SA Reiterstandarte (a brown-shirt riding unit) and subsequently joined the Nazi cavalry corps.[6] When confronted by reporters in February 1986 about these memberships, he said: "But these were purely sports activities and had nothing to do with the (Nazi) party."

Subsequently, in a formal memorandum submitted to the U.S. Department of Justice on 12 April 1986, he explicitly stated that he was not a member of either organization. Since then clear documentary evidence to the contrary has surfaced. In a personal questionnaire that he had filled out in 1940 when applying for a court position, Waldheim himself listed membership in the

National Socialist Student League as of 1 April 1938 and in the SA Reiterstandarte as of 18 November 1938. This document was reproduced in the 4 April 1986 edition of the *National Zeitung,* a neo-Nazi newspaper published in Munich.

Waldheim was thus able to study law at the University of Vienna and diplomacy at the Consular Academy. One of his Academy classmates was George Weidenfeld, a Jew who is now Lord Weidenfeld, head of a publishing house that published Waldheim's last book, *In the Eye of the Storm.* Following the Anschluss in 1938, Weidenfeld fled Austria for England, but he renewed contacts after the war and kept them up. Weidenfeld, in an affidavit dated 15 June 1987 wrote that during the time they were at the Consular Academy together (1937–1938) "Kurt Waldheim was generally known as an active liberal Catholic and convinced anti-Nazi, who came from a conservative-Catholic milieu, voiced definitely anti-racist views and had many Jewish friends."

In 1936, at age eighteen Kurt received orders to report to an Austrian cavalry unit for induction and training, after which he was put on the Austrian army's reserve list. He was called up again in 1938, this time for service in the German army following the Anschluss.

In the Eye of the Storm depicts the German army as less Nazi than the civilian world. Waldheim writes: "A civilian whose politics were under scrutiny was better off as a soldier. The uniform was protection against the Gestapo and the Nazis. Our family was still under constant police surveillance; my father was detained briefly from time to time and we were always being questioned. We lived in daily apprehension, but in the army there was much less harassment of those known to disapprove of Nazism, and I had no further trouble." He says that anti-Nazi literature was circulated freely "and I read it all." He also reports that Sunday mass was always well attended and it "provided us with a rallying point and a means of maintaining our opposition to the notoriously anti-religious politics of the regime."[7]

This description of anti-Nazism in Hitler's German army was written more than forty years later, when Waldheim was denying any links to the Nazis in his past and before the disclosure of his army service in the Balkans. There the units with which

he served, mainly as an intelligence officer, committed egregious war crimes (murder of Yugoslav civilians, executing of captured commandos, and deportation of Jews from Salonika to concentration camps). Certainly there were some non-Nazis and anti-Nazis in the army, and there was indeed a plot by military officers to oust Hitler in late 1944, but there is no evidence of such widespread anti-Nazi feelings in the German Army of 1938 as Waldheim suggests.

Waldheim was able to return to Vienna to complete his studies at the Consular Academy in the spring of 1939. He then studied law with great intensity and passed the basic examination in the spring of 1940. Shortly thereafter the 45th Reconnaissance Unit was called up for service, this time in France, where his diplomatic manner and command of French served the Germany occupiers well. In December 1940 he was commissioned as a reserve lieutenant.

When Hitler ordered the German invasion of the Soviet Union on 22 June 1941, Waldheim's cavalry unit was part of the invading force. For his efforts in the taking of Brest-Litovsk Lieutenant Waldheim was awarded the Iron Cross, Second Class. His combat activities continued until December, when a piece of shrapnel ripped through his right leg.

After surgery in a field hospital in Minsk and two months of physical therapy in Vienna, Waldheim was assigned in March 1942 as an intelligence officer with German forces in Yugoslavia. Because he spoke Italian as well as French, Waldheim was dispatched to an Italian division in Montenegro as a liaison officer. He was subsequently assigned to the quartermaster unit of the German 714th Infantry Division, which had the main role in a bloody "purification action" against Yugoslav partisans at Kozara, where between 66,000 and 68,000 Yugoslavs were killed in action, executed after capture, or deported. For his role in the battle Waldheim received from Ante Pavelic, leader of the Nazi-dominated Croatian regime, the silver medal of the Crown of King Zvonimir with Oak Leaves.

In the latter part of 1942 Waldheim obtained leave to resume his law studies in Vienna. He was promoted to First Lieutenant on 1 December. He yearned for a career as a lawyer and a diplomat, was willing to work hard for it and apparently would let nothing stand in the way.

Returning to active duty in April 1943, Waldheim was assigned to the German Ninth Army liaison staff in Tirana. He served as interpreter between Italian and German officers. He also translated Italian army papers into German.

Assigned in July to the German liaison staff in Athens, as deputy operations officer, Waldheim again served as interpreter with the Italian army commands. He also had to read and initial the large number of reports from German units in the Balkans and route them to the appropriate German and Italian commands. Consequently, he had to be aware of the atrocities being committed by the Nazi forces against civilians in the Balkans and the deportation of Greek Jews to the death camps.

In October Waldheim rejoined the intelligence section (IC/AO) of Army Group E (12th Army) at Arsakli, Greece. He enjoyed a personal relationship with the group commander, General Alexander Lohr, later convicted of war crimes by a Yugoslav war crimes tribunal and executed. Lohr, also an Austrian, enjoyed intellectual discussions with Waldheim. Lohr had represented Austria at disarmament talks in Geneva, and this made him particularly interesting to Waldheim, intent on a diplomatic career. Moreover, Waldheim usually went out of his way to cultivate those of higher rank or with power.

In February Waldheim was granted medical leave in Austria. He was thus able to complete his dissertation and be close to his fiancée, Elizabeth (Cissy) Ritschel, who was also a law student. She had become a member of the Nazi party and had left the Catholic church. She rejoined the church in 1944, and they had a Catholic wedding in August of that year.

Cissy, a tall, striking brunette was the daughter of Wilhelm Ritschel, an illegal (Austrian Nazi) since 1934. At the time of the Anschluss in 1938 he was a cell director for the Austrian Nazi party. In October 1940, Cissy, then eighteen, applied for membership in the Nazi party and three months later became a member. An intelligent, ambitious and hard-working woman, she became a significant asset to Waldheim in his diplomatic career.

Waldheim's dissertation was on Konstantin Frantz, a nineteenth century German political theorist with anti-Semitic, pan-German ideas. This was a clever choice for an ambitious Austrian during the Nazi period. His dissertation sponsor, Professor Alfred Verdross,

had a worldwide reputation as an expert on international law. Verdross, an ambitious opportunist, had supported Dollfuss and Schuschnigg in their struggle for a conservative, independent Austria, but he moved quickly to ingratiate himself with the Nazis after the Anschluss.

Frantz's pan-Germanism had an appeal for the Nazis, but Waldheim's dissertation focused on Frantz's advocacy of federalism, with the various peoples of the federation enjoying autonomy. The geographic boundaries of such a federation would resemble those of the Holy Roman Empire. The federation would be peaceful, not the result of conquest. While this idea of peaceful federation was clearly contrary to the Nazi program of military conquest, Waldheim deftly concluded his dissertation by arguing that the Third Reich was saving Europe by its struggle against the non-European world. His dissertation was accepted, and he received his doctorate on 14 April 1944.

Waldheim then returned to duty with Army Group E in Greece. The German army was carrying out brutal, massive attacks against civilians and taking hostages in reprisal for Greek partisan operations against the Germans. Whole villages were destroyed. In the opinion of some officers, including Waldheim, this indiscriminate slaughter was counterproductive. Toward the end of an intelligence report on 23 May 1944, Waldhem wrote: "The *reprisal measures imposed in response* to acts of sabotage and ambush have, *despite their severity*, failed to achieve any noteworthy success, since our own measures have been only transitory, so that the punished communities or territories soon have to be abandoned once more to the partisan bands. On the contrary, exaggerated reprisal measures undertaken without a more precise examination of the objective situation have only caused embitterment and have been useful to the bands. It can be demonstrated that the population broadly supports the bands and supplies them with excellent information" (the italics are Waldheim's own).[8]

Also during Waldheim's service in Greece, the command of Army Group E ordered the deportation of all Jews from its territory. More than 60,000 were deported. Waldheim claims that he knew nothing of the mass deportations at the time; they were carried out by a different section of the headquarters staff under the direction of the Abwehr chief, Major Friedrich Wilhelm Hammer.

An International Historians Commission set up by the Austrian government to investigate the charges against him concluded that, as an intelligence officer at the headquarters of the units involved, he knew about the criminal activities and did not try to stop them. It also concluded that, while Waldheim had no command authority, he had "repeatedly assisted in connection with illegal acts and thereby facilitated their execution." The Commission challenged Waldheim's statement that "resistance against the ordering power would have been suicide from the outset." It stated: "Latest research has turned up no example of a soldier refusing to take part in the murder of civilians being brought before a military court and punished."[9]

One of the historians on the Commission, Professor Yehuda Wallach, expressed particular skepticism about Waldheim's statement that he knew nothing of the deportation of Jews from Salonika at the time he was in Greece. Wallach noted that Arsakli, where Waldheim was stationed, was only a few miles from Salonika. Almost a quarter of Solonika's population was Jewish, and it would have been impossible to go from Arsakli to the German recreation facilities in Salonika without passing the area that had been largely Jewish and noticing that it had been emptied. Wallach also observed that Waldheim, though only a first lieutenant, had substantial input into the intelligence estimates on the basis of which targets were selected for attacks and destruction by the German army; his superior in rank, a major, was lazy and left most of the work to Waldheim.[10]

When asked by Finger during a 1988 interview why his books described in detail the hardships he, his family and Austria had suffered during World War II, but made no mention of Austrian Jews, Waldheim said: "I wanted to survive. I was no hero. An Austrian I knew was hanged for listening to BBC."[11]

(Austria had a prewar population of 200,000 Jews; now it has only 6,000. Nearly 70,000 died in concentration camps and more than 20,000 fled the country or were imprisoned.)

A panel of five judges who convened in connection with an HBO television program on 5 June 1988, concluded that, while Waldheim had knowledge of the atrocities committed by German army units with which he served, "the evidence which has been put before us is not enough to make it probable that

Lt. Waldheim committed any of the war crimes alleged against him in this inquiry."

The television program prompted a most interesting commentary in *Encounter* by C. M. Woodhouse, former commander of the Allied Military Mission to the Greek Resistance. He opined that, given the terms in which the issue was presented, the panel was correct in concluding that Waldheim was not a major war criminal. But Warren went on to describe Waldheim's "fabrication of a mendacious report" on the interrogation of one of his commando officers, Captain D.A.F. Warren which "made it doubly sure that Warren would be murdered." Investigation of the Warren affair may yet reveal information that will further embarrass Waldheim. Woodhouse also describes a number of instances in which Hitler's order that all captured commandos be executed was ignored or evaded by German officers, who were not themselves punished by execution. Further, he describes the case of General Lanz, commander of the XXII Mountain Corps Group in Northern Greece in 1943, who disobeyed an order from Hitler to execute some 6,000–7,000 prisoners.[12] Once again, Waldheim's excuse that resistance against orders would have been suicide comes into serious question.

Robert Herzstein, after a searching inquiry, concludes that "while Waldheim assisted many individuals who fell into the war-criminal category, he was not a war criminal himself. Rather, he was a bureaucratic accessory to both the criminal and the legitimate military activities of Ic/AO." He writes:

> So far as I have been able to determine, Kurt Waldheim did not in fact order, incite or personally commit what is commonly called a war crime. But this non-guilt must not be confused with innocence. The fact that Waldheim played a significant role in military units that unquestionably committed war crimes makes him at least morally complicit in those crimes. Lawyers and judges can debate the legal niceties. The historian sees Waldheim as having served as a small but very real cog in a large, murderous machine.[13]

Our own conclusion is very close to Herzstein's. We have seen no conclusive evidence to date that Waldheim ordered or personally

committed a war crime, but he was definitely a bureaucratic accessory. Whatever qualms he may have had about the Nazi crimes in the Balkans, he did nothing to stop or impede them. Indeed, he was part of the deadly machine. The intelligence reports he processed included information used by Nazi military authorities in identifying targets for destruction and war crimes.

Waldheim has never provided an adequate explanation of why he concealed his wartime service in the Balkans. The German version of his book, *In the Eye of the Storm*, does have two brief sentences about it. "Upon termination of my study leave and after recovering from my leg injury, I was recalled to army service. Shortly before the end of the war I was in Trieste." The English version stated only that, because of his injury on the Russian Front late in 1941, he was "discharged from further service at the front." It made no mention of any further army service.

Waldheim explains the difference by stating that Weidenfeld, the publishers of the English version, were already impatient about the fact that publication was substantially behind schedule and that the manuscript was already too long; consequently, they refused to add the material from the German version. (The original manuscript was in English, but the German translator made some significant additions and alterations.) This may be technically true, but there was certainly space to mention his wartime service in the original manuscript if he had merely shortened some of the descriptions of his early life that were far less significant. When one also considers Waldheim's later evasions and misrepresentations in answer to specific questions on his wartime service described in chapter 3, it is hard to avoid the conclusion that the omission was deliberate, designed to serve his ambition.

Indeed when on 8 April 1988, we interviewed Brian Urquhart, who as undersecretary general for special political affairs was Waldheim's top political adviser, Urquhart said that Waldheim lied to him "at least twenty times" about his wartime record.

After the German armies of the Balkans crumbled in 1945, Waldheim managed to make his way to Cissy in Romsau, Austria, in territory controlled by the Western Allies. There on 7 May, two days before the German surrender, their first child, Lieselotte, was born.

Shortly thereafter Waldheim was demobilized and reported to an American processing center in Schlamding. There, because of his service as an intelligence officer, he was placed in a truck with other former Wehrmacht officers and taken to a POW camp near Bad Tolz, an American Army interrogation center. He was released in mid-June.

Political developments in Austria then helped to pave the way for Waldheim's diplomatic ambitions. In November 1945 the Austrian People's Party (formerly the Christian Social Party in which the Waldheims were active during the thirties) won a majority. Its leader and the new chancellor, Leopold Figl, was an old acquaintance of Walter Waldheim. Figl had been a staunch supporter of Dollfus and Austrian independence and had spent six years in the Dachau concentration camp. He appointed as undersecretary of state for foreign affairs Karl Gruber, a dynamic man of thirty-six who had been active in the anti-Nazi Resistance and had the confidence of U.S. intelligence officers. As his political aide, Gruber chose Fritz Molden, still in his twenties, who had worked for the American OSS during the war and subsequently married the daughter of OSS Chief Allen Dulles. When Waldheim applied for a job at the Foreign Ministry, Gruber asked Molden to check Waldheim out and the latter, after consulting his friends in American intelligence, told Gruber that there was nothing negative.[14] Consequently, Waldheim received a provisional appointment as attache. Molden was impressed by Waldheim's enthusiasm, dedication, and meticulousness.

Waldheim's next hurdle was the denazification program, under which more than half a million Austrians were to be screened. Originally under the Allies Denazification Bureau, the program was turned over to the Figl government in January 1946. In a prepared statement Waldheim asserted that he could not have completed his studies without joining the National Socialist German Students League and that he could not have entered his legal career without membership in the S.A. Riding Corps. He also submitted a notarized copy of the Nazi 1940 description of him as a supporter of the Schuschnigg regime ''who gave proof of his hostility, towards our movement by sounding off.''[15] The special commission, overloaded with cases and facing a deadline of 30 June 1946, never resolved Waldheim's case. (In

fact, about half the cases before the commission were never re-solved.) On 19 June the Foreign Ministry retrieved his dossier from the commission and appointed Waldheim a career member of the Austrian Foreign service, retroactive to 1 June. In November he was officially informed that he would not be subject to any penalties arising from Nazi affiliations and would not be required to register with the government as a former Nazi.

Early in 1947 the Big Four deputy foreign ministers met in London and agreed to consider a Yugoslav claim to more than 300,000 square kilometers of southern Carinthia and Styria, along with Austria's response thereto. Gruber argued that the Big Four had already agreed that Austria should resume her 1937 borders, including the disputed territories, and that it made no sense either geographically or politically to divide Carinthia. The Soviets, who had their own dispute with Vienna over the definition of German assets in Austria, which the Soviets wanted to remove as reparations, initially supported the Yugoslavs. Subsequently, however, the Soviets made it clear that they had no real concern with the Yugoslavs' territorial claims. Waldheim served as an aide to Karl Gruber, who represented Austria on the Austrian Treaty Commission.

In the spring of 1947, the Yugoslavs began to direct attention to the intelligence branch of army Group E, and found that Waldheim had served on it. They decided to try to embarrass Gruber, whose anti-Nazi record was impeccable, by bringing charges against his aide, Waldheim, before the U.N. War Crimes Commission in London. Their problem lay in coming up with acceptable evidence of Waldheim's personal responsibility for war crimes. Nevertheless, in order to beat a 1 March 1948 deadline set by the War Crimes Commission, the Yugoslavs presented their charges against Waldheim on 13 February 1948. The Commission held its last session on 26 February and, with a long agenda, agreed without discussion or dissent to put Waldheim's name on the UNWCC list as an Abwehr officer charged with war crimes, including murder. Subsequently, his name was also included in the Control Registry of War Criminals and Security Suspects, compiled under the direction of the Allied Control Commission.

The Yugoslavs made no attempt to have Waldheim extradited. Apparently they wanted to surprise and embarrass Gruber at the

Big Four deputy foreign ministers conference held in London, February–April 1948. But on 14 January, a month before the conference began, Waldheim had been transferred to the Austrian Legation in Paris. Though Gruber has stated that the transfer was made routinely and with no knowledge of the Yugoslav charges against Waldheim, his assertion is hard to believe. It was an inconvenient time for Waldheim to move to Paris—midwinter and his wife almost six months pregnant. Also, it is doubtful that the work in Paris was as important to Austrian interests as Waldheim could have been at Gruber's side in London; he had, after all, been involved in the negotiations from the beginning.[16] In any case, the transfer spared both Gruber and Waldheim potential embarrassment.

Waldheim had another stroke of luck. As a result of Tito's break with Moscow, Yugoslavia became more concerned to have good relations with Austria and by July 1948 decided it was no longer in its interest to pursue Waldheim's case. Gruber, who had been their antagonist on the territorial dispute, now became one of their important conduits to the United States. He was the first non-Communist foreign minister to visit postwar Belgrade and got along very well with Tito—as did Waldheim in the 1970s when, as secretary general of the United Nations, he visited Tito. By that time the Yugoslavs may have had more evidence against Waldheim but no interest in pursuing the matter.

In November 1951 Waldheim returned to Vienna to become chief of the personnel division in the Ministry of Foreign Affairs. When the American Embassy requested a biography of Waldheim, there was no mention of either wartime service or his doctoral dissertation. It is surprising that no one in the Embassy or Washington raised questions about the gap of several years in view of Waldheim's age when the war started. One of this book's authors (Finger) served at the American Consulate General in Stuttgart in the latter 1940s and wrote biographies on virtually all the leading political figures in Southwest Germany. In every case he was able to dig up voluminous material about their activities during Hitler's twelve-year rule, including the war. Why was no similar effort made in Waldheim's case? (He had mentioned wartime service in the Balkans in his 1945 application for the Austrian Civil Service and in the accompanying curriculum

vitae.) Was he protected by Gruber and the latter's excellent relations with U.S. authorities? Was he valuable to American intelligence because of his wartime experience with German units
fighting Tito's partisan army? Were U.S. government parties so
preoccupied with the Cold War that they were willing to overlook
dubious activities during World War II, as was the case with the
Nazi scientists?[17]

On the basis of documentary evidence and interviews with
many of the principals, Herzstein concludes:

> Throughout the postwar period, including his tenure as UN
> secretary-general, Kurt Waldheim was a U.S. intelligence
> asset who expected to be—and always was—protected by
> his friends in the American intelligence community.

> Waldheim's relationship with American intelligence began
> in May 1945 when he was shipped off to the POW camp
> at Bad Tolz for debriefing by G-2 (U.S. military intelligence).
> The previous month the OSS had provided G-2 with a list
> of German officers considered to be "of interest" to the
> United States. Having served as a Wehrmacht intelligence
> officer in Yugoslavia, Waldheim would no doubt have been
> on that list, for the OSS was hungry for the information
> about the "Yugoslav" secret intentions and methods.[18]

The foreign ministry, of course, was run (in 1945–1948) by Karl
Gruber and his assistant, Fritz Molden—both of whom had
worked for American 430th Counter-Intelligence Corps. Among
their main concerns was keeping Communists from taking control of the newly reorganized ministry. They were also under instructions to provide their American friends with information
about the Soviets and the Yugoslavs. In such an environment it
would have been unthinkable to employ anyone—particularly a
personal secretary—whom the Americans didn't trust. The fact
that Gruber and Molden hired Waldheim with only the most cursory investigation into his background could mean only one thing:
he had aready been vetted by U.S. authorities.

In the early years of the Cold War, Waldheim's firsthand
knowledge of Tito's partisan army—which at the time was

considered to be the main East Bloc threat to Austria and the West—made him increasingly valuable to the Americans. Certainly he was too valuable to be allowed to fall into Communist hands. After all, in addition to his Balkan expertise, there was his undoubted knowledge of Gruber's and Molden's activities on behalf of the U.S. Counter-Intelligence Corps.[19]

Adding fuel to this suspicion is the CIA's reluctance to release information about its files on Waldheim. In 1987 the World Jewish Congress filed a Freedom of Information Act request with the CIA for any information in its files on Waldheim. On 9 June 1987 the CIA replied that only "one . . . was located, an OSS report dated 26 April 1945." It should be noted that the date of this document was about two weeks before Waldheim was taken to Bad Tolz for interrogation, suggesting that the trip to Bad Tolz was no accident.

On 21 June 1988, *The New York Times,* in an article entitled "CIA and Waldheim," reported that "in the files of the Central Intelligence Agency there is a psychiatric profile of Kurt Waldheim dating from the 1970s, when he was Secretary General of the United Nations." Thereupon the World Jewish Congress again wrote the CIA, asking why material in its possession was withheld from public knowledge, particularly since the WJC had made a specific request a year earlier. In its replay dated 29 June 1988, the CIA explained that its earlier letter referred only to OSS files. It also stated that it would "neither confirm or deny the existence of any CIA records responsive to your request." Thus, the questions of how much Washington knew about Waldheim's past and of his possible association with American intelligence services at some period of his career remains partially unanswered, at least for now.

Waldheim's next post was in New York. In 1955, he came to the United Nations as the Austrian observer. He and Cissy were gracious hosts and guests in the U.N. diplomatic circle, smiling and good mannered, taking care to cultivate people who might be important to them.

In 1956 Waldheim became Minister to Canada, in charge of the Austrian Legation in Ottawa. At his instigation diplomatic relations were upgraded to the embassy level in 1958, and Waldheim became, at age thirty-nine, a full-fledged ambassador.

In 1959 he became a father for the third time. The Waldheims had two daughters, Lieselotte and Christa, and a son, Gerhard, the middle child. He took a great interest in the children, saw that they went to the finest schools and often pulled strings on their behalf. Most notable was the case of his oldest, Lieselotte, who was already in the U.S. Secretariat when he became secretary general but advanced in rank more rapidly than most.

Also in 1959 Bruno Kreisky became Austria's Foreign Minister. Kreisky was a passionate Socialist, Jewish and anti-Zionist. Because the Socialists and the Austrian People's party were then and for many years linked in a coalition government, Kreisky found it expedient to advance the career of Waldheim who, while not then a party man, was considered a conservative "clerical." In 1960 Kreisky appointed Waldheim director-general of political affairs in the Foreign Ministry.

Waldheim returned as permanent representative to the United Nations in 1962. He carefully cultivated not only the major powers but also the representatives of the Third World, who increasingly came to dominate the proceedings of the General Assembly. To them he emphasized that Austria, too, was neutral in the Cold War. When the U.N. Committee on Outer Space was formed, he became its chairman. Peter Thacher, the U.S. representative to that committee in the 1960s, described Waldheim as pleasant and discreet but extremely tenacious in pursuit of his objectives.

Waldheim returned to Vienna in 1968 to become foreign minister in a cabinet headed by conservative chancellor Josef Klaus. In August the Soviet Union and several of its Warsaw Pact allies invaded Czechoslovakia to crush the "Prague Spring." Waldheim, anxious not to antagonize the powerful Soviets, ordered Ambassador Kirchschlaeger in Prague not to grant too many visas to Czechs who wanted to leave. Kirchschlaeger, sympathetic to the plight of the would-be refugees, defied Waldheim's orders and issued emergency visas to many desperate Czechs. Waldheim did not attempt to stop any of the refugees from entering Austria nor did he take disciplinary action against the defiant Kirchschlaeger.

In 1979 Bruno Kreisky's Socialists won a narrow electoral victory and Kreisky became Chancellor of a minority Socialist cabinet, leaving no place for a nonparty foreign minister. Waldheim then

returned to New York as permanent representative and began a campaign to succeed U Thant as secretary general when the latter's second term ended on 1 January 1972.

Meanwhile the conservative Austrian People's party asked Waldheim to be its candidate for the ceremonial post of president, which had always been held by Socialists. Despite his lack of experience in domestic politics and representing a party that had never won the presidency, Waldheim polled an impressive forty-seven percent of the vote. This result added to his stature as a candidate for secretary general. Moreover, he had the full support of Cancellor Kreisky, who mobilized his international Socialist contacts on Waldheim's behalf. Waldheim resumed his cultivating of Third World representatives and made a strong effort with the five permanent members, each of which had the veto power on the required Security Council recommendation to the General Assembly. His campaign culminated in a Security Council resolution of 21 December, 1971, recommending to the General Assembly that he be appointed secretary general.

What kind of man was the new secretary general? Certainly hard working, tenacious, discreet, meticulous with protocol and bureaucratic details, resilient, determined and possessed of uncommon stamina. Yet his determination is driven more by laser-beam ambition than by dedication to principles. As he would show in his ten years as secretary general, he was painstakingly polite and cordial, even obsequious, with those he wanted to cultivate, but arrogant and often insensitive to Secretariat staff (to be detailed in chapter 5). He was shrewd but not intellectual. He listened to classical music, loved to acquire fine paintings and silver, but was not deeply cultural. He had been a devoted husband and father, but was considered dull by many colleagues. He could be earthy but loved pomp and ceremony. He was vain and eager for recognition and publicity. He moved cautiously and carefully, protecting his rear, and went to great pains to please those he wanted to cultivate. He was careful not to show his emotions in public. All in all, an excellent bureaucrat from whom one could expect few surprises, who could be depended upon not to make waves. (These represent not only our personal views but a consensus garnered from scores of interviews with people who knew and worked with Waldheim.)[20]

How could such a man, a former officer in Hitler's German army, be elected to head an organization dedicated to the high principles enunciated in the U.S. charter? Did Moscow, Washington, London, and Paris know about Waldheim's service in the Balkans with the units that were committing war crimes? Since this information was available to all four governments, was it provided to the officials who made the decisions about whether to accept Waldheim as secretary general? Why did the responsible government agencies not make a thorough background check? Or, if they did, why did they ignore his wartime record? Did any of the governments use the information to blackmail Waldheim? These are some of the questions we shall delve into in our next chapter.

Chapter 2

Electing a Secretary General: Accentuating the Negative

The General Assembly, consisting of the 160 Member States, appoints the secretary general. But the United Nations charter stipulates that it do so on the recommendation of the Security Council (fifteen members). That is, in fact, the crucial hurdle. There each of the five permanent members (China, France, the United Kingdom, the Soviet Union, and the United States) has a veto that can block any candidate. Beyond that hurdle it has been clear sailing. Each candidate recommended by the Security Council has been appointed secretary general by the Assembly.

This power to bar a candidate has been used by various permanent members to serve their political interests. The first secretary general, Trygve Lie, was accepted by the Soviets at a time when there appeared to be no viable alternative. Some forty of the original fifty-one members, including twenty from Latin America, were friends or allies of the United States. The Soviets knew the West would not agree to a candidate from their bloc. Lie, a social democrat who came out of Norway's trade union movement, was accepted. Stalin did not think much of the United Nations anyway, and the Soviets could use their veto to stop any unwelcome action in the Security Council. Also, the Soviets were given the post of assistant secretary general for political and security affairs, their main concern in the United Nations. This

post proved to be of very limited influence. Successive secretaries general, knowing that the Soviet assistant secretary general was an instrument of his government, have used two assistant secretaries general for special political affairs to advise them on policy, carry out delicate political missions, and run peacekeeping operations. For many years one of these was Ralph Bunche, who acted as a true international civil servant, did not take instructions from the U.S. government, and did not hesitate to differ with Washington when he thought the United States was wrong. Others have been British and Latin Americans, carefully chosen to be truly internationally minded and objective. (In the early 1960s both of these posts and the Soviet position were redesignated as under secretary general.)

Soviet calculations went awry in 1950. On 24 June, the North Koreans invaded South Korea. When the Security Council met on 25 June the Soviet seat was empty. Moscow was boycotting the Council on the grounds that the Chinese seat was illegally occupied by the representative of Chiang Kai Shek, who in 1949 had been chased off the mainland by the forces of the People's Republic of China. But the boycott proved to be a self-inflicted wound, depriving the Soviet Union of its veto.

Lie provided the Council with reports from the U.N. Temporary Commission on Korea confirming that North Korea had initiated an all-out invasion. That same day, 25 June, the Council, with the Soviets absent, adopted a resolution denouncing the action as a breach of the peace, calling for the cessation of hostilities and the withdrawal of the North Koreans, and calling on members to render every assistance to the United Nations in the execution of the resolution. Two days later the Council adopted a U.S.-sponsored resolution recommending that the member states "furnish such assistance to the Republic of Korea as may be necessary to repel the armed attack and to restore international peace and security in the area."[1]

On 7 July the Council, on U.S. initiative, adopted resolution 588 requesting that the United States establish a U.N. United Command, designate the commander (General Douglas MacArthur), and report to the Council as appropriate. Again, the Soviets were absent. Sixteen nations provided contingents for the U.N. Command, but the bulk of the forces were American and South Korean.

The Soviet representative returned to the Security Council in August when he became, by rotation, president of the Council. With the threat of the veto restored, the United States moved in the General Assembly a resolution dubbed "Uniting for Peace" (Resolution 377, 3 November 1950), which adopted procedures enabling the convening of an emergency special session of the General Assembly to consider threats to international peace and security if Council action was blocked by a veto.

In line with resolutions of the Security Council and the General Assembly, Trygve Lie used his position and the Secretariat to support the U.N. forces in Korea against the Communist North Koreans. The Soviet assistant secretary general had no power to block or impede such activities. Not surprisingly, the Soviets turned bitterly against Lie and vetoed his reappointment when he completed his five-year term in December 1950. The United States, in turn, made it clear that it would veto any other candidate. So the Security Council was deadlocked.

The United States, which could then count on a comfortable majority, moved in the General Assembly to extend Lie's term. He continued in office for two more years, during which time he was boycotted by the Soviets and their allies; they noted that the secretary general, under Article 97 of the charter, could be appointed by the General Assembly only upon recommendation of the Security Council.

The impasse was ended by agreement among the major powers on Dag Hammarskjöld, then Sweden's minister of finance. Mild-appearing, soft spoken, coming from neutral Sweden, and with a background of finance, Hammarskjöld must have appeared safe to the Soviets. To their surprise he turned out to be a man of deep convictions, daring, and with a messianic belief in the need for an effective United Nations. Accordingly, he stretched the powers of his office to the limit. In 1958, when the Security Council failed to act on his request to enlarge the U.N. observer Group in Lebanon, Hammarskjöld announced to the Council that he felt obliged to go ahead with the enlargement, in order to fulfill his responsibility for the maintenance of international peace and security—and he did, without serious objection from the members.

But the final straw for the Soviets was the U.N. Operation in the Congo (ONUC). The U.N. force had originally been sent in after

a request by Patrice Lumumba, then Prime Minister. During a coup by Colonel Mobutu (now President Mobutu of the country, renamed Zaire) in September 1960, Hammarskjöld's representative in Leopoldville (now Kinshasa), Andrew Cordier, closed all airports. He stated that he did so in order to hold down the level of violence. But, since troops supporting Lumumba were in Stanleyville, the effect was to tip the scales in favor of the coup. Subsequently, Lumumba, a leftist, was executed.[2]

The Soviets, who saw Lumumba replaced by a government friendly to the United States were furious. Appearing at the General Assembly in the fall of 1960, Nikita Krushchev demanded Hammarskjöld's resignation. The secretary general, bolstered by support from non-aligned countries as well as most Western nations, declined. The Soviets also proposed that the secretary generalship become a troika, with one representative each from the East, the West, and the non-aligned, and with each of them having a veto over action. This proposal, too, was successfully opposed, and Soviet bitterness against Hammarskjöld remained. He was also disliked by Belgium and by Western mining interests (Union Miniere), which opposed his use of the U.N. force to suppress the separatist movement in the Katanga, the center of mining operations, in order to unify the country.[3] But most Western countries, particularly the United States, and most non-aligned countries were content to "let Dag do it." In protest, France, the Soviets, and other Easten Europeans refused to pay their assessments for ONUC.

The controversy over Hammarskjöld's bold concept of the powers of the secretary general was halted by his tragic death in a plane crash en route to Katanga in September 1961. But his actions certainly accentuated the Soviet distrust of an activist secretary general, which was an important and perhaps the key factor in their support of Waldheim rather than Max Jakobson of Finland in 1971. The latter, as permanent representative of Finland, had shown himself to be activist and dynamic, raising the prospect that as secretary general he might take actions contrary to Soviet interests.

Hammarskjöld's successor, U Thant of Burma (now Myanmar), managed to maintain the acceptance of all parties, though he did

irritate President Johnson and Secretary of State Dean Rusk by his outspoken criticism of the U.S. war in Vietnam. As he finished his second five-year term in 1971, Thant announced that he would retire. The Soviets, feeling comfortable with Thant, urged him to remain, but he declined. In fact, Gromyko, the Soviet foreign minister, refused to believe the Soviet Mission's reports that Thant would not accept another term until he spoke personally with Thant in September 1971.

The Soviets then supported Gunnar Jarring, Sweden's ambassador to Moscow, and thus a known quantity. Jarring made no effort to gain support, apparently because of a Nordic Group decision to support Max Jakobson of Finland.

Still, there was no dearth of candidates; there were at least ten. After a week of periodic meetings, on 16 December the five permanent members narrowed the list down to six: Filipe Herrera of Chile, Max Jakobson of Finland, Gunnar Jarring of Sweden, Sadruddin Aga Khan of Iran, Kurt Waldheim of Austria, and U Thant. At the insistence of the nonpermanent members, the names of Endel Kachew Makonnen (Ethiopia) and H. Shirley Amerasinghe (Sri Lanka) were added.

Other names that surfaced ephemerally were Terence Nsanze (Burundi), Majid Rahnema (Iran), Janez Stanovnik (Yugoslavia), Maurice Strong (Canada), Perez Guerrero (Venezuela), Aga Shahi (Pakistan), Sridath Ramphal (Guyana), and, as possible interim secretary general, Constantin Stravropoulos (Greece) and Roberto Guyer (Argentina).[4]

Herrera was backed by China, which wanted for political reasons to show support for a Third World country (Allende's leftist government in Chile), but was opposed by the United States, which favored Jakobson. The Soviets favored Jarring, whom China opposed, and the French Sadruddin who was opposed by the Soviets. Waldheim was not the first choice of any major power. The deciding factor was not who was best qualified for the post, but who could avoid a veto, a process of negative selection.

On 16 December 1971, the Council decided to vote by secret ballot. Jakobson was highly upset at the Council's decision, taken at the initiative of the Soviet representative, Yakov Malik. He believed that no major power would oppose him openly, since

their arguments against him would not stand up to the daylight. A secret ballot would enable a permanent member to use the veto anonymously, with no need to justify its position. A phone call from President Kekkonen the next day indicated that he, too, feared the impact of a secret ballot and "was very angry at the incompetence of the supporters of my candidacy." Jakobson called Secretary Rogers, urging that he give his attention to the voting procedure, but Rogers appeared to have more serious concerns on his mind.[5]

Jakobson may have had some justification for believing that an open ballot would have improved his chances, but he was mistaken in believing that an open ballot was the normal procedure. The record shows that an open ballot on the election of a secretary general was usually taken only when informal consultations had indicated that there would be no opposition. An exception occurred in October 1950 when votes on Trygve Lie and a Polish candidate were taken by a show of hands; Lie was vetoed by the Soviets, and the Pole failed to get the required seven votes. A few days later proposals to elect Charles Malik of Lebanon or Carlos Romulo of the Philippines were also defeated. Following the deadlock in the Council the General Assembly extended Lie's term, but as indicated earlier, he was boycotted by the Soviets.

In March 1953, with three candidates, the Council used a secret ballot, and none emerged successfully. But, at its meeting of 31 March the Council agreed on Dag Hammarskjöld and voted by a show of hands, ten in favor and one abstention. The president announced that, "while a secret ballot would have been normal it was unnecessary in view of the fact that all members of the Council had made their position clear in statements made in the course of the meeting." Again, in the case of U Thant, his nomination as acting secretary general and then as secretary general was approved unanimously, by open voting. U Thant's second term was approved by the Council after a statement by the president, without a vote. This information was provided to all Council members on 15 December 1971, before they decided on a method of voting.[6] Under the circumstances, with no agreed candidate, it is not surprising that the Council decided on secret ballots.

After meetings of the five permanent members, the U.S. Mission to the United Nations (USUN) proposed to the State Department that it be authorized to vote "yes" on Jakobson and Sadruddin, that either the United States or the United Kingdom should vote "no" on Thant if he appeared to have nine votes and "abstain on the remainder unless soundings show likelihood of nine votes coupled with no veto."[7]

It should be noted that USUN's request would have meant vetoing Waldheim. Moreover, despite Jakobson's misgivings about George Bush, then the U.S. permanent representative—which we shall discuss later—Bush participated in the five-power discussions and signed the telegram proposing these voting instructions. In the five power meetings Bush also urged that voting be done by a show of hands but went along with an apparent majority view that the vote should be secret. The suggestion of a veto of U Thant, who was the favored candidate of the Soviets, should also be noted. Thant's repeated outspoken criticism of the U.S. war in Vietnam may have been a factor.

In reply, the State Department instructed Bush to vote for Jakobson and Sadruddin, abstain on Waldheim and vote against all other candidates, presumably including Thant. Significantly, these instructions would have left the door open for Waldheim had there not been a veto by a permanent member.

It is also significant that these instructions required a veto of Felipe Herrera, the Chilean candidate, apparently because the U.S. disapproved of the then government of Chile, headed by Salvador Allende. Yet Herrera had been a distinguished representative of a variety of Chilean governments considered friendly to the United States. He had been governor for Chile on the Board of Governors of the IBRD (World Bank), 1953–1958; executive director of the International Monetary Fund, representing six South American countries, 1958–1960; and president of the Inter-American Development Bank, 1960–1971. Perhaps it was short-sighted to block Herrera because the Allende government proposed his candidacy; his service as secretary general would have continued long after Allende's fall. This is not to argue against support for Jakobson, who was superbly qualified, but rather to question whether Waldheim was a better fallback than Herrera.

Since the voting was secret, the tallies that follow are based on reporting by the USUN.

On the first ballot, 17 December, the results were as follows: Amerasinghe 5 yes, 6 no, 4 abstentions; Herrera 7–4–4; Jakobson 8–5–2; Jarring 7–5–3; Makonnen 4–6–5; Sadruddin 3–5–7; Waldheim 10–3–2. Only Waldheim had the required nine votes, but at least one of the negative votes on him must have been by a permanent member, evidently China. U Thant's name was removed prior to the vote, because he had sent a letter to the president of the Security Council asking that his name be excluded from consideration.[8]

The next day at a five-power meeting it was decided to recommend that the Security Council vote on the four candidates who had received seven or more votes on the first ballot (Herrera, Jakobson, Jarring, and Waldheim) plus Issafou Djermakerkoye (Niger), Carlos Ortiz de Rosas (Argentina), Sridoath Ramphal (Guyana), Terence Nsanze (Burundi), and Gabriel Valdes (Chile). Subsequently, the nonpermanent members of the Council added Majid Rahnema (Iran), while Terence asked to have his name removed. Bush again suggested an open ballot at the five-power meeting but was "immediately and firmly opposed".[9]

The Security Council took its second ballot, in secret, on 20 December. At the suggestion of Japan, Amerasinghe of Ceylon (now Sri Lanka) was added to the list of nine candidates. The results were as follows: Amerasinghe 4 yes, 6 no, 5 abstain; Djermakoye 5–8–2; Herrera 7–6–2; Jakobson 9–5–1 (Soviet veto); Jarring 7–4–4; Ortiz de Rosas, 10–3–2 (Soviet veto); Rahnema 3–8–4; Ramphal 3–7–5; Valdes 7–5–3; Waldheim 11–2–2 (Chinese veto). Although the veto was announced only in the case of the three candidates who received nine or more votes, USUN noted that at least one permanent member had voted against every one of the ten candidates.[10]

Prior to the vote USUN had been instructed to abstain on Ramphal and vote no on all other candidates except Jakobson, Waldheim, and Ortiz. Rahnema was specifically mentioned as an undesirable candidate who "might just squeak by with nine positive votes." These instructions clearly left the door open for Waldheim if China dropped its veto. Ironically, the telegram was drafted by the late Martin Herz, an unusually able and experienced

career foreign service officer who was born in Austria. Herz was then deputy assistant secretary for International Organization Affairs. The draft was cleared by his superior, Samuel de Palma, by Richard Pedersen, counsel of the State Department who had spent some fifteen years at USUN, and by the acting secretary of state; thus, the telegram reflected a collective judgement, with input from USUN.[11] Yet even Herz, with his astuteness and his Austrian origin, was apparently unaware of Waldheim's wartime record. Having served at the American Embassy in Iran for a number of years, he must have had good reasons for doubting Rahnema's suitability.

Meeting again on 21 December, the Security Council, by a vote of 11-1-3, recommended to the General Assembly that Waldheim be appointed secretary general. Ortiz received twelve affirmative votes and Jakobson nine, but they were both vetoed by the Soviets.

USUN reported that it was "surprised(!) to learn that the one negative vote had not been that of a Permanent Member and, consequently, Waldheim had obtained the required majority." But USUN expressed some satisfaction that "whatever the faults, if any, of Jakobson campaign, Finns by putting well-qualified candidate in the field early and maintaining him to the end helped ensure that Soviet first choice, U Thant, would not be reelected."[12] True, but the United States could have blocked either Thant or Waldheim with a veto.

That same day USUN delivered to Waldheim the following message from the secretary of state:

> Please accept my warm congratulations on your nomination to the post of Secretary General of the United Nations. In the exercise of the duties of that office, which will place great demands on your diplomatic talents, courage, and experience, you will have the best wishes of the United States as well as our strong support and cooperation. Rogers.[13]

Bush himself telephoned to offer congratulations but was unable to get through because the Austrian Mission to the United Nations was flooded with calls. Since Waldheim was destined to serve as secretary general for at least five years, it is not surprising that the United States offered congratulations.

Waldheim attributes China's decision to stop vetoing him to an approach made in Beijing by Hans Thalberg, then Austria's ambassador to China. Thalberg, careful of Chinese sensitivities, tried to make delicate allusions to Austrian hopes but found no opportunity to mention Waldheim's name to Premier Chou En-lai. Thalberg returned to his hotel utterly downcast. He learned only after Waldheim's election that Chou had been most impressed at Austria's tact and discretion. "Supposed failure has in fact been success."[14]

The judgment of Waldheim and Thalberg about the reasons for China's change of position involves some speculation. There could have been other factors, including the possibility that China, which had taken its seat at the United Nations only three months before and which tended to move cautiously at that time, might have been unwilling to be perceived as blocking the election of a secretary general only days before the office would become vacant. In any case, China had already made its political point by its support for a Third World candidate. (In 1981, China maintained its veto, forcing Waldheim to abandon his quest for a third term.)

Jakobson was bitter about losing and has blamed the United States. He asserts that William Rogers, then secretary of state, told him in the Spring of 1971 that the State Department, having studied the matter carefully, had reached the conclusion that Jakobson was the only acceptable candidate. The others were either unacceptable for political reasons or not competent for the job, with Waldheim specifically mentioned as being in the latter category. He also states that on 1 October 1971, in official discussions with the Finnish foreign minister, Rogers said that "the US will vote for your candidate and shut down any other." He says he was present at that discussion, along with two other Finnish Ambassadors, Munki and Hyvarinen.[15]

Rogers denies that any such pledge of a veto was made. He preferred Jakobson, considering Waldheim too oily and obsequious.[16] In separate conversations Joseph Sisco, who was assistant secretary of state, and Richard Pedersen, who was counselor of the Department—both with long experience at the United Nations and consulted by Rogers on U.N. matters—denied any U.S. veto commitment to Jakobson. They said they liked Jakobson and

considered him preferable to Waldheim but felt that Waldheim was acceptable. After all, he had been foreign minister, had served for many years at the United Nations, had been Chairman of the U.N. Outer Space Committee, and was considered friendly to the United States.[17] Both they and Rogers stated that they had had no knowledge of Waldheim's wartime record in the Balkans. Rogers remarked, somewhat ingenuously, that he had assumed the background check would be done by the United Nations. Sisco and Pedersen, with their background and experience, must have known that the U.N. Secretariat could not do a background check on a candidate for the post of secretary general; apparently Rogers never raised this question with them. Yet Waldheim's name was on a list of alleged war criminals against whom charges had been filed with the U.N. War Crimes Commission—a list maintained in the U.S. Government archives in Washington. The UNWCC files themselves were in U.N. custody in New York, readily accessible to the U.S. Government on request.

There is clearly a contradiction between Jakobson's account of Rogers promise of a stubborn veto of Waldheim and the denial by Rogers, Sisco, and Pedersen. In an effort to resolve this contradiction, and to obtain other information for this chapter, we requested, under the Freedom of Information Act, the declassification of all 1971 telegrams and memoranda dealing with the subject of elections from the State Department or the U.S. Mission to the United Nations (USUN). After a year of waiting, we received copies of more than 200 such communications, and many of these were very helpful in preparing this chapter. But we did not receive a copy of the record of the meeting on 2 October 1971, between Rogers and the Finnish foreign minister at which, according to Jakobson's book, Rogers promised a protracted veto of Waldheim. It is not likely that such an important meeting would not be recorded in the State Department and reported by telegram to USUN and the American Embassy in Helsinki. Yet repeated efforts to get this record were to no avail.

Jakobson is convinced that, if the United States had steadfastly vetoed Waldheim, the Soviets would have finally accepted Jakobson. His president, Kekkonen, had excellent relations with the Soviet leadership, and Jakobson hoped he would bring them around if the deadlock could be maintained a little longer.

But recently reports have surfaced indicating that perhaps the official Finnish campaign was not, after all, totally and enthusiastically committed to Jakobson at all levels of the Government and throughout the election process. Interesting although somewhat anecdotal pieces of evidence tend to support this view.

A Ph.D. student in the Graduate School of the City University of New York, Tapio Kanninen of Finland, interviewed Max Jakobson in August 1984 in Helsinki for the research he was conducting for Professor Finger in connection with his studies on the role of the secretary general and on the question of enhancing his capacity for early warning and preventive diplomacy. He also asked Jakobson's reaction to a personal experience indicating that President Kekkonen might have himself, at some point in time, thought about his own possibilities of becoming the U.N. secretary general.

Academician Kustaa Vilkuna, the husband of Kanninen's aunt, was one of President Kekkonen's best friends, if not the best one. In the 1960s Kanninen remembered Dr. Vilkuna coming home directly from the president's sauna, from a very small gathering of his closest friends, saying to his wife, a son and Kanninen that President Kekkonen has just expressed interest in becoming the secretary general of the United Nations. When his son challenged him, Dr. Vilkuna said firmly that President Kekkonen wants to manage not only Finnish affairs but the whole world's affairs. Confronted with this inside information in 1984 Max Jakobson was evidently somewhat surprised but did not take it seriously. At that time he did not believe it affected the outcome of the 1971 election of the secretary general.

This memoir becomes more interesting when juxtaposed with another piece of new information. Andrei Gromyko gave an interview for Finnish TV in the spring of 1989 in Moscow. As reported in the biggest newspaper in Finland, *Helsingin Sanomat,* on 22 September 1989, Gromyko said that the Soviet Union had nothing against Max Jakobson, as a person, for election to the office of the secretary general in 1971. The Soviet Union could well have supported the election of Jakobson had the contacts from the Finnish aide not been that "formal and unenthusiastic." The article also mentions that the contacts in the USSR on Jakobson's campaign for the office were handled solely by President

Kekkonen at that time. Max Jakobson stated in the same article that Gromyko's statement is important, since it came from Gromyko and was prepared by him and carefully thought out. We doubt whether the Soviets would have accepted Jakobson even if a deadlock had been prolonged and Kekkonen had intervened more forcefully in Moscow. They did not want a dynamic, forceful secretary general. They were quite willing to have someone less brilliant, but malleable and unlikely to make waves that might be contrary to Soviet interests. Gromyko's statement, coming eighteen years after the crucial 1971 election, raises interesting questions about the election but may have been made to mollify the Finns and, consequently, may not represent conclusive evidence of the Soviet position on Jakobson's candidacy in 1971.

There are a number of indications that Soviet opposition to Jakobson was deep-rooted. At a lunch given by the Thai permanent representative to the United Nations on 16 December 1970, a Norwegian reporter asked Victor Lessiovski, a Soviet assistant to the secretary general, about Jakobson. Lessiovski replied that the Soviets would not support Jakobson for secretary general even ''if Kekkonen crawled down Red Square to request it.'' Lessiovski then commented that, while Jakobson himself was not a Zionist, his parents had taken part in Zionist activities, and no one with a Zionist tint, no matter how pale, could expect to be secretary general.[18] A year later Vernon Mwanga, the permanent representative of Zambia, called on the Soviet ambassador, Yakov Malik, for the express purpose of urging, as a spokeman for the non-aligned, that the Soviets reconsider their veto of Jakobson; he argued that Jakobson was clearly the best of the candidates. It is interesting that Mwanga spoke on behalf of the non-aligned members, which include more than twenty Arab states. Mwanga reported that Malik acknowledged the validity of this reasoning but was noncommittal and not encouraging.[19] Further, Arkady Shevchenko, who had worked closely with Foreign Minister Gromyko in 1971, was convinced that Moscow would not have accepted a dynamic and independent man like Jakobson.

Nor is it likely that a deadlock would have put pressure on the Soviets. If no one had been elected before 31 December, Thant would in all likelihood have served ad interim, and that was what

they really wanted. They were instructed to vote for Waldheim if no better candidate emerged, and they did. Foreign Minister Gromyko had little respect for Waldheim and was reluctant to call on him as "a waste of time" when he was in New York for annual sessions of the General Assembly.[20]

The situation was, in many ways, the reverse of 1950, when the United States maintained its position of vetoing all challenges to Secretary General Trygve Lie. The resultant deadlocks then meant that Lie, on the recommendation of the General Assembly, continued in office, as the United States wanted. A deadlock in 1971 would probably have meant that Thant would stay in office ad interim; this the Soviets wanted, while the United States clearly did not.

Another indication of the Soviet wariness was their attitude toward the candidacy of Sadruddin Aga Khan, who had done a very creditable job as high commissioner for refugees. A KGB official in the U.N. Secretariat, Victor Lessiovski, told Fereydoun Hoveyda, who was Iran's permanent representative to the United Nations in 1971, that the Soviets could not accept Sadruddin because he was not really from Iran (the Aga Khan family is based in Geneva); consequently, the Soviets could not put pressure on him through the Iranian government.

As for the Soviet's second choice, Gunnar Jarring, he was known among Nordic diplomats as extremely cautious and reticent. Since he was Sweden's ambassador to Moscow, the Soviets knew this very well.

Of course the Soviets did not want to offend the Finns unnecessarily, particularly not their friend, President Kekkonen. Consequently, they never came out openly against Jakobson and probably did leave the Finns with the impression, deliberately, that they might accept him. During the course of 1971, they sowed the report that the Arabs would not accept Jakobson because of his Jewish background. The Finns checked with the Arab states and found that some of them—notably Syria and Iraq—did try to develop a common negative Arab position, but they did not succeed. Most Arab states wanted to avoid an anti-Semitic posture.[21] Mwanga's approach to the Soviets, noted above, is another indication that Arab opposition was not a serious factor.

On its side, the United States, while preferring Jakobson, was no longer as gung ho about an active United Nations as it had been a decade earlier. With the admission of about a hundred new members, mostly from Asia, Africa, the Pacific, and the Caribbean, the Third World had taken control of the agenda and the resolutions of the U.N. General Assembly. The Africans focused much of their attention on South Africa, often to the discomfort of the West. The Arabs, with twenty-two members in the Afro-Asian group, found it easy to get majority support for anti-Israel resolutions, again to the discomfort of the United States. Also, the new nations continued to use the U.N. General Assembly to bring pressure on the industrialized countries to provide more aid and trade opportunities.

Moreover, at the White House, where Nixon and Kissinger were the architects of American foreign policy, there was little regard for the United Nations. Their focus was on relations with the two Communist giants, China and the Soviet Union. Samuel De Palma, assistant secretary of state for International Organization Affairs 1969–1973, quotes Kissinger as saying: ''Don't bother me with that UN crap.''[22] Kissinger's memoirs about the years 1969–73, *The White House Years*, ran over 1500 pages, but there is not one word about the 1971 election of the secretary general nor about the United Nations's role in international politics. In that context it is not surprising that the Nixon White House, which called the shots on foreign policy, should have little concern about the choice of a secretary general, except to block any candidate who was politically unacceptable or might take initiatives damaging to American interests. Waldheim, the candidate of friendly Austria, might not be dynamic or brilliant, but he was not likely to do anything damaging to American interests. The question of his wartime record did not come up.

Evidently senior U.S. officials believed in December 1971 that the Soviets would not relent in their opposition to Jakobson. According to Richard Pedersen, counselor for the State Department at the time, President Nixon and the British Prime Minister, who met in Bermuda in December 1971, considered that the Soviets would not change. Accordingly, they decided to drop any attempt to block Waldheim. Moreover, the French foreign minister, Maurice Schuman, urged Rogers to support Waldheim because

Jakobson did not speak French.[23] This may not have been an important consideration for the United States, but it was one more factor.

It may also be worth noting that there was not much warmth between Jakobson and George Bush, who was then the U.S. permanent representative to the United Nations. If Bush had been enthusiastic about Jakobson, he might have intervened on his behalf with the White House. There is no indication that he did so. Bush was annoyed by Jakobson's active support of the People's Republic of China during the Assembly's earlier consideration of the issue of Chinese representation, though Jakobson was acting on instructions from his government. The United States had lost in its move to have both Chinas seated, despite the most vigorous efforts of Bush and his staff.

In this connection it is interesting to note how differently Jakobson and Waldheim evaluated Bush. Jakobson writes:

> When George Bush arrived in New York he was not knowledgeable about international politics and he did not attain, in my view, in terms of intellectual or professional capabilities, the level of the previous permanent representatives I had known. (Some of my American friends told me later that I would not hide this view from Bush; if so, it was, of course, a mistake on my part.)[24]

In contrast, Waldheim writes:

> Bush is an engaging, open-minded man. His popularity at the United Nations and during his many foreign missions was based on his absolute integrity, his superior grasp of foreign policy fundamentals and his attractive low-key manner. He has certainly been a valuable spokesman for his government in dealing with a host of international issues.[25]

These quotes reflect personal chemistry that could not have been helpful to Jakobson in his quest for a U.S. veto against Waldheim, whose wartime record was not the main issue.

So the major powers and the membership at large accepted Kurt Waldheim as secretary general, not as a great leader but as

someone who would probably work conscientiously and would not rock the boat. Indeed, he was reelected in 1976 and would have been reelected for a third five-year term if the Chinese had not, for their own political reasons, maintained a veto against him. They were supporting Salim Salim of Tanzania as a way of showing their solidarity to the Third World. And no government raised the question as to whether a former officer in Hitler's German Army should hold the highest position in the United Nations, without even a background check.

Clearly government attitudes had changed significantly since 1945. The report of the Preparatory Commission of the United Nations stipulated in Paragraph 57: "The Secretary General should take the necessary steps to ensure that no persons who had discredited themselves by their activities or connection with Fascism and Nazism shall be appointed to the Secretariat." This stipulation was incorporated, as Staff Rule 56, in the Provisional Staff Regulations issued in 1948 (SGB/8; 25 June 1948), which read: "No persons shall be appointed who have discredited themselves by their activities or connections with fascism or nazism."[26] It was, in effect, repealed in 1952 when the General Assembly adopted new Staff Regulations.[27]

Even if the original regulations had remained in effect, they would not have been applied to the choice of secretary general; they envisage appointments *by* the secretary general, who presumably would do the necessary screening. The choice of the secretary general himself is up to the governments, who bear the full responsibility.

The United Nations charter itself provides criteria which governments should have taken to heart in choosing a secretary general in 1971 and should take more seriously in the future. Article 101 states: "The paramount consideration in the appointment, transfer or promotion of staff shall be the necessity for securing the highest standards of efficiency, competence and integrity." Apparently, the government officials who supported or acquiesced to Waldheim's appointment did not know of the extent to which he had concealed or lied about his wartime record. But it is difficult to understand why they did not make a more thorough background check, given his nationality and his age at the time World War II broke out.   .

Even the government of Israel, which would normally be most sensitive about a former German army officer, appears to have raised no questions with other governments. A search of all telegraphic correspondence between USUN and the State Department in 1971 revealed no mention of any Israeli approach, which would certainly have been reported therein if it had been made. Nor is there any indication that the Israelis raised the issue of Waldheim's wartime record or his conduct as secretary general when he was reelected in 1976, a year after the General Assembly adopted the infamous resolutions equating Zionism with racism. Nor did they raise it in 1981, when only a Chinese veto blocked Waldheim from a third term. Conversations with Israelis who were in responsible positions during that decade also indicated that Israel had not raised the issue with the United States or any other government. Perhaps the answer lies in the response of Ambassador Ovadia Soffer, who was with the Israeli Mission to the United Nations in the 1970s. "He was the least bad of the bad."[28] Israel may have feared that a secretary general from Africa or Asia would have been more prejudicial to their interests.

An insight into the waning interest of goverments in Nazi activities as the Cold War waxed is suggested by their attitudes toward opening the files of the U.N. War Crimes Commission (UNWCC). When the UNWCC, a body independent of the United Nations, was dissolved in 1948, its archives, to the extent that they were not returned to the governments which had provided the material, were placed in the custody of the United Nations. At that time rules for access were drawn up by the U.N. Secretariat, in consultation with the Legal Adviser and the former chairman of the commission. Under these rules a large part of the material was made available for "serious research." However, the individual charge files were subject to restrictions "in order to preserve their confidentiality as they contain information which, for the most part, has not been communicated to the individuals concerned and not subject to judicial evaluation." This restriction also applied to the lists of war criminals, suspects, and witnesses; related indexes; and the formal charges and related papers. These restricted records could be inspected and used only for official United Nations purposes, meaning the prosecution of war crimes. Access was granted only to governments for that

purpose upon written request and on the understanding that the records were strictly confidential and were to be handled on the same basis of confidentiality as any other material being used in a criminal investigation.[29]

These rules for access remained unchallenged by any government for thirty-seven years. Then, in May 1986, Ambassador Benjamin Netanyahu of Israel addressed a letter to the secretary general, Javier Perez de Cuellar, requesting him to ''take the immediate steps necessary to ensure free access to the general public to all the material stored in the archives of the United Nations War Crimes Commission.''

Netanyahu's move was made on his own initiative. Following public revelations of Waldheim's wartime activities, Netanyahu informed the government of Israel that he intended to examine the files of the U.N. War Crimes Commission, then in U.N. custody, for information on Waldheim. He took along members of his staff who could read the various languages involved in the documents and made photostatic copies of relevant materials. In the process he noticed the thousands of files stored in the building and decided to request free access to all of them. Again, the Israeli government did not object to his proposed action.[30]

Perez de Cueller decided that any changes in the rules should be made only after consultation with seventeen governments that had been members of the UNWCC. (The Soviets had been invited but refused to join.)

The first consultation revealed that most of the governments were reluctant to change the rules to provide wider access to the files. Initially, only Australia gave its agreement, followed by the Netherlands and Yugoslavia. Then the Israelis, with a nod from the secretary general, went public. For a year and a half they lobbied for the other governments and fed the press, especially *The New York Times*. A decisive factor was U.S. support, after which most of the other governments fell into line. Most reluctant were Poland and France, the latter contending that the files should remain closed until 100 years after the death of the individual concerned. Perhaps the French were aware that the files contained charges against many of their nationals, including some who might be currently involved in French politics. This might explain their reluctance to see a Pandora's box opened, particularly since

some of the charges, which had not been investigated, might have been false and malicious.

Meanwhile, the secretary general had been taking the heat from those who wanted the files opened. Finally, he indicated that, unless the rules were changed, he would hand all the files back to the governments concerned. In due course, having ascertained that no government would protest vehemently, he went ahead with liberalizing access.

It is now possible for scholars as well as government officials to go through the files, "fishing." What is required is a letter to the secretary general from the permanent representative or permanent observer, transmitting an application from a national or permanent resident of his country and attesting that the application meets the criteria specified for access to these records. The letter must also affirm that the applicant will abide by the rules, which specify that no copies may be made and make clear that the files are largely based on hearsay and have not gone through the judicial process. If the applicant proceeds to publish material based upon information obtained from these files and not available from the proceedings of international or national tribunals, the applicant undertakes to insert a statement that the records may include unsubstantiated information and hearsay evidence. The applicant also accepts full responsibility for any claims that may arise from the use of such material.

During an interview in 1988 we asked Waldheim whether he was aware that his dossier was in the UNWCC files and whether he had been concerned about it. He said he was not concerned, because he considered himself to have been anti-Nazi.[31]

Clearly the U.S. Government now takes a different position. In the Spring of 1986 Attorney General Edwin Meese III decided that Waldheim should be placed on the Watch List, which would bar him from entering the United States. Such action had never before been taken against a head of state. This action was based on a 1978 amendment to the Immigration and Naturalization Act sponsored by Congresswoman Elizabeth Holtzman. This denies admission to the United States of any alien who, in the view of the attorney general, "had initiated, assisted or otherwise participated in the persecution of any person because of race, religion, national origin or political opinion" between 23 March 1933 and

8 May 1945. This action against Waldheim had been recommended by the Office of Special Investigation (O.S.I.) in Meese's Justice Department. Prodding and supplying the OSI with materials and documentation was the World Jewish Congress, which had undertaken a massive investigation and exposure of Waldheim over many months.

As of this writing no such action had been taken by Yugoslavia, even though the overwhelming majority of the victims of the German Army's war crimes in the Balkans were Yugoslavs. This inaction is congruent with Tito's long term policy of giving priority to Yugoslavia's current national interests which, to his mind, made good relations with Austria and Waldheim more important than Waldheim's role in World War II. Tito's successors appear to be maintaining this policy.

Nor is Yugoslavia's focus on current national interests rather than World War II crimes unique. There is ample evidence that the United States, the Soviet Union, Britain, and France have frequently done the same. Christopher Simpson has documented many American programs that recruited former Nazis and Nazi collaborators, including war criminals, for scientific research, espionage, propaganda, subversion, and guerrilla warfare in Soviet dominated areas of Europe. This knowledge of the areas, contacts, experience, and ruthlessness appealed to those Americans who ran destabilization and espionage programs as part of the Cold War. In many ways the higher the official, the more useful he appeared to be, even though he might be a man with major responsibility for war crimes. These activities were sanctioned and abetted by high officials in the State Department, the CIA, and the Immigration and Naturalization Service. Those recruited and protected included the infamous Klaus Barbie, "the Butcher of Lyons" and other major war criminals. Similar programs were carried out by the Soviets and the British as the Cold War waxed and grew more intense.[32]

Chapter 3

Waldheim as Secretary General

In evaluating Waldheim's service as secretary general, we endeavored to avoid being prejudiced by his wartime record. We did investigate to see whether his actions toward delegates and Secretariat staff were anti-Semitic or anti-Israel. We also looked into allegations that his wartime record was used by the Soviets, the Yugoslavs, or the British to blackmail him. We found no evidence that his actions at the United Nations were anti-Semitic, nor that he was personally anti-Israeli, nor that he was blackmailed. We shall examine each of these questions in what follows. We shall not, of course, confine our discussion to these questions alone. Rather, we shall examine the entire spectrum of his activities during his ten years as secretary general.

It may be well at this point to outline briefly the functions and powers of a secretary general and the limitations on his powers, which are far short of those wielded by the president or prime minister of a country.

The United Nations charter itself gives very limited authority to the secretary general. Article 97 designates him as "the chief administrative officer of the Organization." Article 98 states that he "shall act in that capacity at all meetings of the General Assembly, of the Security Council, of the Economic and Social Council, and of the Trusteeship Council, and shall perform such

other functions as are entrusted to him by these organs.'' It further calls on him to make an annual report to the General Assembly on the work of the Organization.

Taken literally, these articles would make the secretary general little more than an administrator carrying out instructions from the General Assembly, Security Council, Economic and Social Council, and Trusteeship Council, and reporting to the General Assembly. The only other authority specifically accorded to him is in Article 99: ''The Secretary-General may bring to the attention of the Security Council any matter which in his opinion may threaten the maintenance of international peace and security.'' To date this authority has been used very sparingly. Generally these threats are brought to the attention of the Council by a concerned member state. Also, in the past, the secretary general has been reluctant to bring a situation to the attention of the Council if his initial informal soundings indicated that such a move might be counterproductive. Moreover, when these informal consultations indicated that a member state was prepared to bring the issue to the Council, the secretary general has preferred that it do so.

In terms of resources, the secretary general's powers are also very limited. He has no standing military forces at his command. Indeed, he does not even have an official plane at his disposal and must usually fly by commercial airliner or charter. The regular budget of the United Nations is less than one-tenth of one percent of the federal budget of the United States.

Yet the office of secretary general, skillfully used, has had a significant influence on many world events. A secretary general who is respected by governments and the media for his competence, judgment, and integrity can have substantial impact.

From the beginning there have been conceptual differences among member states. The Soviet Union has generally insisted that the secretary general limit his functions to administration, although Gorbachev has suggested a stronger role for him as the Soviets have begun advocating a more active role for the United Nations.[1] The United States and most other member states have considered that Article 99 gives the secretary general implied political powers above and beyond his purely administrative functions. This difference in concept was reflected in the American

preference for Jakobson, who appeared more dynamic, and the Soviet preference for Jarring or Waldheim, whom they considered more cautious and predictable.

In fact, however, every secretary general has gone beyond mere administration and has been active on political issues. We have already discussed the political activities of Trygve Lie and Dag Hammarskjöld. Hammarskjöld, in addition to his role in the Congo which infuriated the Soviets, took a number of other noteworthy initiatives. He openly espoused the representation of the People's Republic of China in the United Nations, despite strong U.S. opposition. At the same time he interceded in Peking to assist in the release of American flyers held by China. Hammarskjöld organized and provided guidelines for the first U.N. peacekeeping force, in the Sinai in 1956. This established precedents for all future operations of U.N. peacekeeping forces. In 1958 the Security Council was unable to agree on the expansion of the U.N. Observer Group in Lebanon, and Hammarskjöld stated that he would nevertheless increase the size of the Group to what he considered necessary. Subsequently, he told the General Assembly that he considered it the duty of the secretary general to take action, even in the absence of instructions from the Security Council or the General Assembly, should this appear to him necessary in order to help in filling any vacuum that may appear in the systems which the charter and traditional diplomacy provide for the safeguarding of peace and security."[2] U Thant expressed a similar view. "Two simple considerations are inescapable. First, the Secretary-General must always be prepared to take an initiative, no matter what the consequences to him or his office may be, if he sincerely believes that it might mean the difference between peace and war. In such a situation the personal prestige of a Secretary-General—and even the position of his office—must be considered to be expendable. The second cardinal consideration must be the maintenance of the Secretary-General's independent position, which alone can give him the freedom to act, without fear or favour in the interests of world peace."[3]

Despite Soviet abstention on the Security Council resolutions authorizing the U.N. peacekeeping operation on Cyprus, Thant organized the force (UNFICYP). On the other hand his public criticism of U.S. involvement in Vietnam angered President

Johnson. Perhaps his most controversial action was the speedy withdrawal of the U.N. Emergency Force (UNEFI) from the Sinai in 1967, at the request of President Nasser, which contributed directly to the commencement of hostilities between Israel and Egypt.

Kurt Waldheim though careful to avoid controversy offending the major powers, nevertheless took some diplomatic initiatives. In 1973, on the basis of a broad authorization from the Security Council he prepared a full blueprint for the organization of UNEF II. In 1980 he made an unsuccessful visit to Teheran in an effort to free American hostages.

Javier Perez de Cuellar, a quiet and discreet man, was very successful in 1988 in mediating an end to the fighting between Iran and Iraq, facilitating the withdrawal of Soviet forces from Afghanistan, and in getting an agreement to bring about independence for Namibia. He also has been involved in efforts toward a peaceful settlement in Western Sahara and in Cambodia.

There are many reasons why all five secretaries general, despite differences in backgrounds and personalities, have been more than chief administrators. First, resolutions of the Security Council often provide instructions to the secretary general that are broad and ambiguous. Many times this is the only way to obtain agreement among representatives whose instructions from their governments are not fully congruent. The need to interpret and implement these resolutions gives broad latitude to the secretary general, particularly in organizing and managing peacekeeping operations or negotiations aimed at political settlements and conflict resolution. He must, of course, be keenly aware of the limits of tolerance of the member states; for example, a state may at times tacitly accept actions that it is not willing to endorse openly.

Second, the Security Council is sometimes deadlocked when action is needed, for example, Lebanon in 1958 when Hammarskjöld took the necessary action without authorization by the Council. Third, member states frequently are impelled to ask the secretary general to provide good offices or mediation in crisis situations, without a formal resolution of the Security Council or the General Assembly. Fourth, he has the benefit of a knowledgeable staff, which can bring incipient crises to his attention and provide expertise for dealing with them. Fifth, he can appeal to world

opinion through the media, as U Thant did on Vietnam. Sixth, he can influence the less visible but most important activities that relate directly to people, centered at U.N. agencies in Geneva. Finally, a secretary general of recognized integrity wins the trust of governments which encourage him to become involved in dealing with major political issues. It is an important political vehicle to be put at the service of the member states, large and small, in dealing with problems of serious concern to them.

It should also be noted that the annual report to the General Assembly, called for in Article 98 of the charter, has been used by each secretary general not only to report on the activities of the United Nations but also to survey the world situation and to call attention to problems and serious situations. Such reports, and particularly the Introduction to them, are read carefully by governments. This has an impact on the governments and has frequently resulted in their taking initiatives or actions in efforts to deal with the issues presented.

Thomas Franck has described these political activities as "The Black Box Function" of the secretary general. He writes:

> Rather like prime ministers and presidents, all the secretaries-general also have regarded themselves as holding a sacred trust, not as merely occupying a political office. . . . Each incumbent has tried to enunciate his record and spell out the historical implications of his more important initiatives in part to lay a firm foundation for the next master-builder.[4]

Kurt Waldheim's Performance: The Political Side

Having looked at the limitations and opportunities of the office, we can now turn to assessment of Waldheim's performance as secretary general.

It was the political side, the maintenance of international peace and security, that interested him the most. Here he was aided by experienced, competent deputies, notably Brian Urquhart and Roberto Guyer. Urquhart, British, had been with the Organization from the beginning. He had been deputy to the late Ralph

Bunche, who was in many ways the father of U.N. peacekeeping. Bunche had received the Nobel Prize in 1950, for his outstanding role in achieving armistice agreements between Israel and its neighbors, Egypt, Syria, and Jordan, whose armies had invaded when Israel proclaimed itself a state in 1948. He had so much confidence in Urquhart that he left him all his papers to do a biography rather than write his own memoirs.

Initially Waldheim was leary of Urquhart because the latter had worked closely with Hammarskjöld and U Thant. In a little while, however, the new secretary general realized how valuable Urquhart's experience and expertise were. Urquhart, on his side, had his doubts about Waldheim, but realized that, as an international civil servant, it was his job to serve whomever the major powers chose as secretary general. He also came to recognize that Waldheim was hardworking and possessed great physical stamina. Moreover, Waldheim was ready to accept ideas and suggestions and follow them up, and he was never too tired or too indifferent to undertake an awkward journey or to make a difficult phone call. They then developed a good working relationship.[5] Urquhart and his staff were involved in every major political decision or action, and this helped significantly in making Waldheim's political actions, when he took them, reasonably effective.

Urquhart also drafted the Introduction and other significant political sections of the secretary general's annual report to the General Assembly. The undersecretary general for Special Political Affairs, Roberto Guyer (Argentina) was assigned important diplomatic missions. Meanwhile, Urquhart continued to run the Office of Special Political Affairs. But it was not until 1974 that he was promoted to undersecretary general, the rank held by Bunche and Guyer. He writes:

> It meant a great deal to me to follow in Bunche's footsteps, and I was also proud to have got to the top in the Secretariat under my own steam, instead of being a political appointee as most of my senior colleagues had been.[5]

This delay of almost three years in Urquhart's promotion and the obvious fact that he had earned it would appear to give the

lie to one rumor; that the British, who had the UNWCC files on Waldheim containing information not only about the German Army's war crimes against Yugoslavs, Greeks, and Jews but also about the execution of a group of British commandos, used the information to pressure Waldheim into promoting Urquhart. We have found no evidence that the Foreign Office in London knew about these wartime activities, anymore than the top State Department officials did. The existence of files in one part of the government does not guarantee that they will be known to other branches.

It should be noted that Urquhart's promotion came after outstanding work by his office in connection with the October 1973 war and its aftermath. It was they who developed the blueprint for a new peacekeeping force in the Sinai (UNEF II), a masterful job that helped to defuse a potential Soviet–United States confrontation, established guidelines for peacekeeping that were accepted by both the Soviets and the United States, and helped to pave the way for the peace agreement between Egypt and Israel. They also developed the plan for the U.N. force on the Golan Heights (UNDOF), which has helped to maintain a solid truce between Syria and Israel.[7] These were major U.N. achievements, and it is not surprising that Waldheim was grateful to Urquhart and his staff for their contributions. (These actions and their significance will be described and analyzed in chapter 4.)

Another factor in Urquhart's promotion was Waldheim's desire to appoint George Davidson, then head of the Canadian Broadcasting Corporation, as undersecretary general for Administration. Davidson had represented Canada at many U.N. meetings, had been president of the U.N. Economic and Social Council and had known Waldheim well when the latter served as Austrian Ambassador to Canada. The post he would take was held by a British national. It would have been impolitic to have two British nationals in the top rank of the Secretariat—no country has. Apparently both the British government and Waldheim realized that Urquhart had earned the rank.

We have dwelt on the Urquhart case because he and the office he headed were the key to Waldheim's activities in the political and security areas. He did not accept their recommendations with blind trust. Urquhart relates: "Working with Waldheim could be

a grind because he insisted on going over and over the smallest details, often going right back to the beginning and starting all over again, so that meetings and conversations frequently dragged on for hours and late into the night."[8] But we are aware of no major political decision Waldheim took that ran counter to the advice he received from Urquhart and his staff. Waldheim did make some political gaffes in off-the-cuff statements to the media, and we shall discuss those later.

This may be a good point to discuss other blackmail rumors. Waldheim appointed a Yugoslav, Rudolf Stajduhar, as his media officer. Suspicious people have suggested that the Yugoslavs, who had made the original charges against Waldheim to the U.N. War Crimes Commission, used the information to blackmail him, including pressure to appoint Stajduhar. The latter refused to be interviewed; however, C. V. Narasimhan, who was Chef de Cabinet at the time Stajduhar was appointed, told us that it was he who recommended Stajduhar on the basis of the qualities the latter had demonstrated while representing the United Nations in India. (Narasimhan, who had also been Chef de Cabinet for U Thant, is not an admirer of Waldheim and had no reason to protect him.)

As for substantive political activities, Yugoslavia had no need to blackmail Waldheim. It is one of the leaders of the "Group of 77," composed of more than 120 non-aligned countries which, by their sheer numbers, dominate the agenda and the resolutions of the General Assembly. The bulk of the resolutions are recommendations which governments are free to ignore and frequently do. In fact, some among the non-aligned have questioned the value of producing such a large quantity of unproductive resolutions, as if the General Assembly were a legislative body—which it is not.[9] And the Soviet foreign minister, in his statement advocating a more effective United Nations, has stressed the value of negotiation and consensus rather than the adoption of Assembly resolutions over the objection of governments whose cooperation would be essential to making them effective.[10]

But certain resolutions adopted by a majority do have an impact. Those giving instructions to the secretary general are binding on him. Then, there are the budget resolutions. Article 17 of the U.N. Charter requires Members to bear the "expenses of the

organization" as apportioned by the General Assembly. The expenses are apportioned among the members in accordance with a negotiated scale of assessment, based mainly on the ability to pay (gross national product and per capita income). With this scale of assessment, members which collectively pay less than 2 percent of the budget can constitute a majority in voting for it. The United States is assessed 25 percent of the budget, the Soviet Union (including the Ukraine and Byelorussia) about half that. While legally obliged to pay, the major powers have on occasion refused. In the 1960s the Soviets refused to pay their assessed share of the expenses for peacekeeping operations in the Congo and Sinai. Though their arrears amounted by 1964 to more than two years of their assessments, the General Assembly did not act under Article 19 to deprive them of their vote. A major factor in this nondecision was the fear of many nonaligned countries that the Soviets, if deprived of their vote, would leave the United Nations, which would then be less of a world organization. In the latter 1980s the United States paid substantially less than it was assessed, causing grave difficulties for the organization and forcing severe economies and retrenchment.[11] It became clear that, while all members have equal voting rights, some are "more equal than others," as in Orwell's *Animal Farm*.

In this area Waldheim consistently argued for savings through fewer meetings, and a reduction in the flood of documents, but this had little if any impact on the General Assembly. On the other hand, the number of high-level jobs increased by 25 percent during his ten year tenure, partly because of General Assembly action and partly because he liked to hand out jobs as a way of currying favor with governments. As a result of the financial crisis of the 1980s, the number of high-level jobs is being cut back, along with a general reorganization and retrenchment of staff.

Another way in which the "non-aligned" majority has been used is in a plethora of anti-Israel resolutions. The twenty-two Arab members in the group are able to persuade the majority to go along with virtually any resolution they want. The fifty plus African nations want their votes on resolutions condemning South Africa and most feel they have nothing to lose by voting against Israel. Moreover, in the 1970s the Arab oil states were flush with money as OPEC succeeded in multiplying oil

prices many fold, and many African states and their leaders hoped to get some of it.

The most egregious example was the infamous resolution equating Zionism with racism (Resolution #3379, 10 November 1975). In that case some moderate African states realized the harm the resolution would do to the U.N.'s public image in the West and tried to sidetrack the action, but the pressure of zealots among the Arabs and radicals, along with the confrontational stance of the U.S. permanent representative, Daniel Patrick Moynihan, brought the issue to a head.[12]

Waldheim foresaw the disastrous impact the resolution would have on Western public opinion. He called in Fereydoun Hoveyda, then the permanent representative of Iran, and pleaded with him to lend his efforts to sidetrack the resolution. He also called the Shah twice, expressing fear that the resolution might ruin the United Nations.[13] He did not, however, take a public stance against it.

Also during that period the Arabs induced the majority in the General Assembly to take actions and adopt resolutions supporting the Palestinians. The most publicized was the appearance of Yasir Arafat before the General Assembly in 1974. That year the president of the Assembly was Algeria's foreign minister, Abdulaziz Bouteflika. He arranged to have on the dais a chair normally reserved for a chief of state, even though the PLO itself did not claim to be a state. A number of Western Europeans, notably Olaf Rydbek of Sweden, approached Secretariat officials to object to this breach of protocol. Finally it was agreed that the chair would remain on the dais but Arafat would not sit in it. A further furor occurred when Arafat raised his arms, revealing a holster around his waist. According to U.N. security officials, the holster was empty. Nevertheless, it was a disturbing spectacle.[14]

In 1975 the General Assembly adopted a resolution calling for the establishment in the Secretariat of a unit to deal with the ''inalienable rights'' of the Palestinians. In successive years Assembly resolutions called for the expansion of the unit until it became a division. Altogether, annual expenses rose to over six million dollars for conferences, studies, and propaganda supporting one side in the Arab–Israeli dispute.[15] Because of the partisan nature of the operation, the United States has consistently deducted its portion (25 percent) of those expenses.

There is no indication that Waldheim initiated or supported these efforts. As secretary general he was obliged to carry out the instructions of the General Assembly, under Article 98 of the U.N. charter. But he could use his own judgment as to where to place the unit, and he put it under the supervision of William Buffum, an American, who was undersecretary general for General Assembly and Political Affairs. Waldheim could just as well have put it in the Department of Political and Security Affairs, headed by a Soviet, or the Department of Trusteeship, Decolonization and Political Affairs, headed by a Chinese. (The redundancy of "Political" in all these titles is a reflection of the secretary general's desire to placate the three permanent members concerned. In fact, the really important political work is done by the two undersecretaries general for Special Political Affairs and their staffs.) By placing the unit on the Palestinians under Buffum, Waldheim could feel comfortable that any effort by the unit to exceed its responsibilities would be checked. At the same time it was a signal to Washington that Waldheim himself did not want the unit to run amuck.[16]

Waldheim was assiduous in cultivating Arab delegates, but that was not unusual. He was assiduous in cultivating all delegates, including the Israelis. Gideon Raphael was given a welcoming lunch by Waldheim, then Austria's representative, when he arrived in New York in 1967 and was again guest of honor at a farewell event only months later. Other Israeli representatives had cordial relations with Waldheim during the 1970s, when he was the secretary general.

Waldheim also made frequent visits to the Middle East to meet with Arab and Israeli government leaders. This is in line with his belief "that it is personalities more than anything else which influence the destiny of the world." This led him to a series of endless travels to meet world leaders, described in his book, *In the Eye of the Storm.* He visited more than 100 countries in his first five years in office. In addition to the learning experience, there is no doubt that he enjoyed the pomp and ceremony occasioned by these visits. As for the leaders, one learns little about them from the vignettes in his book. Similarly, Eric Rouleau, who worked with Waldheim on his earlier book, *Un metier unique au monde* (in the English version, *The Challenge of Peace*), described his

frustration in trying to glean from Waldheim significant insights that might be included in the book.[17]

On one of these trips, on 6 February 1977, Waldheim presented to King Khaled of Saudi Arabia, in Rijadh, the United Nations Golden Peace Medal ''for his significant contribution to International Peace'' (UN Press Release SG/T/732, 7 February 1977). Just what this contribution consisted of was not explained. On the other hand, Waldheim did not attend the funeral for Anwar Sadat, who had made peace with Israel. He did send the head of the U.N.'s European headquarters and a general from UNTSO and was criticized by the Soviets for doing so.

Waldheim had a difficult position in the Middle East, caught between the Soviets, the Arabs, and their non-aligned supporters on one side and Israel and the United States on the other. He made his own life more difficult by his tendency to travel and make indiscreet public statements, often off-the-cuff.

Following Israel's successful rescue of hostages by a successful raid on the airport at Entebbe, Uganda, he was asked for his comments on the Israeli action. He said, imprudently: ''I haven't got all the details, but it seems to be clear that Israeli aircraft have landed in Entebbe and this constitutes a serious violation of the sovereignty of a Member State. . . .'' On reaching Frankfurt he issued a statement expressing satisfaction over the fact ''that it proved possible to save these human lives.''

Waldheim also committed a much publicized faux pas during a visit to Yad Vashem, the Holocaust memorial, in Jerusalem 30 July. At the entrance to Ohel Yizkor, the ''Tent of Remembrance,'' he was handed a skullcap to cover his head but refused to take it. To explain his refusal, Waldheim said ''I came here as Secretary General of the United Nations and in my own way I honor the Jewish people who have suffered so much.''[18]

Israel regarded these incidents as significant but relatively minor compared to matters of national interest, such as the U.N. peacekeeping forces in the Sinai and on the Golan Heights. With this perspective Israel was not anti-Waldheim during his ten years in office. The Israelis realized that he was under instructions from a General Assembly that was blatantly pro-Arab and made a clear distinction between the office of the secretary general and its peacekeeping operations on one side and the Assembly and

Security Council on the other. Indeed, they even praised Waldheim, who, feeling flattered, issued press statements about the distinction Israel made. Urquhart urged him to avoid such public statements, which could cause problems for him with other governments.

Ovadia Soffer, an ambassador with Israel's Mission to the United Nations during the 1970s called Waldheim the "least bad" of the candidates in 1976. The Israelis did not want Salim of Tanzania or any other African as Secretary General, given Third World support of the Arabs. They knew Waldheim tried to please everybody and did nothing to stop the onslaught against Israel in the General Assembly, but believed that an African or Asian secretary general might even abet such an onslaught.[19] Israel did not oppose Waldheim in any of his three campaigns for Secretary General either in Washington or at the United Nations.

On repeated occasions Arab countries and their allies have tried to exclude Israel from meetings of U.N. organs. Whenever possible Waldheim spoke out against such an approach which, he feared, might put at risk the very existence of the United Nations. He was apparently aware of strong feeling among the American people and their Congress.

Waldheim undertook one initiative that might be considered pro-Israel. He attended the Munich Olympics in 1972 and was appalled by the terrorist murder of the Israeli athletes. Since no delegation had asked to inscribe the item of international terrorism on the agenda of the General Assembly that fall, Waldheim requested its inscription. His initiative was strongly opposed by the Arab delegations. The item was finally inscribed, but with an amendment proposed by Jamil Baroody of Saudi Arabia concerning the "underlying causes" of terrorism, which effectively derailed the initiative and virtually assured that no meaningful action would be taken.[20] In his book, *In the Eye of the Storm,* Waldheim praises Baroody for this "compromise," which "solved the procedural problem."[21] Does this praise reflect naivete or deliberate obfuscation?

In fact, the ad hoc committee established under the amended resolution had a majority of countries that were more interested in attacking actions of the Israeli government, which they charged were the "underlying causes," than in dealing with the issue

of terrorism. As a result the committee's reports were of little or no value in dealing with the issue of terrorism; however, other U.N. actions, taken independently of this resolution and the committee it established have been quite useful.[22]

Chapter 4

Waldheim, the Soviets, the United States, and the Non-Aligned

From an American viewpoint, the major question about Waldheim as secretary general was whether his actions were pro-Soviet or anti-United States. We found no evidence that this was the case. The fact that the United States supported Waldheim's reelection to a third term in 1981—as did the Soviets—would appear to indicate that Washington did not consider him to be biased against the United States.

There have been rumors that the Soviet Foreign Office and the KGB had a file on Waldheim's wartime activities and used it to blackmail him. Here again we found no evidence to support this speculation.

We raised this question in literally scores of interviews with knowledgeable officials who served with Waldheim in the Secretariat and with Americans who worked at high levels in the State Department and at the U.S. Mission to the United Nations. The consensus was that he took great pains not to antagonize the Soviets but that he was just as anxious to please the United States, and that neither country found it necessary to blackmail him.

Arkady Shevchenko, who had been a close aide to Foreign Minister Gromyko before he became undersecretary general for Political and Security Affairs under Waldheim, was certain that

the Soviets did not blackmail him on the basis of his wartime activities. During his own years with Gromyko he saw no indication that the Soviet Foreign Office was aware of the records, nor
did any KGB officials bring the matter up. (Shevchenko defected
to the United States in 1978). He related that Yakov Malik, the
longtime permanent representative of the Soviet Union, would
demand certain jobs for Soviet nationals, not by any reference
to Waldheim's past but rather by saying: "If we don't get these
jobs, you won't be reelected." Such a threat would certainly be
meaningful to Waldheim, and effective, especially since it was
well-known that he used Secretariat appointments as a way of
ingratiating himself with governments. It was also well-known
that Waldheim's overriding interest was to remain secretary
general as long as possible.

According to Shevchenko the Soviets considered Waldheim a
"man of the West" but accepted him because they knew he would
be cautious and not likely to take bold initiatives that might in-
terfere with Soviet objectives. Moscow often complained that the
Secretariat officials sent to conferences in which the Soviets had
an interest were "too low level" and that Waldheim's messages
to such conferences were "not strong enough." The Soviets also
expressed dissatisfaction with the way he ran the World Conference on Disarmament.[1]

Waldheim himself relates that Gromyko never entered into a
substantive discussion with him. Gromyko would ask to see him
once a year before the beginning of the assembly where he would
deliver the Soviets' annual general debate statement but the discussions were "cursory," invariably focussed on disarmament, "but
rarely on other issues of crucial importance." Waldheim continues:
"This was in marked contrast to the extensive and very substantive meetings I had with his American counterparts, whether they
were Kissinger, Cyrus Vance, Edward Muskie or Alexander Haig.
Soon I realized that for Gromyko only one thing counted: power.
That explained by he attached so much importance to Moscow's
relations with the Americans; while painstakingly maintaining the
utmost courtesy, he brought it home to me that power was exactly
what both the United Nations and I myself lacked."[2]

This description dovetails with Shevchenko's observation that
Gromyko had little respect for Waldheim and had to be persuaded

by members of the Soviet Mission to make these brief, perfunctory courtesy calls.[3] Nevertheless, the Soviets did support Waldheim for a second and third term, because they knew what to expect of him and saw no better alternative.

Jean-Francois Giuliani (France), who served as media spokesman for Waldheim, observed that Waldheim was "more afraid of the United States than of the Soviets."[4] Richard Pedersen, who served for fifteen years at the U.S. Mission to the United Nations and was counselor of the State Department during Waldheim's first three years as secretary general stated that Washington considered Waldheim as pro-West.[5] William P. Rogers, secretary of state 1969–1973, observed that Waldheim never did anything "outrageously important." Rogers did not know of anything significant where Waldheim leaned against the United States.[6]

Henry Kissinger, who succeeded Rogers as secretary of state, expressed appreciation to Waldheim for his "unfailingly constructive role" and told him that the United States would fully support his reelection.[7] Of course, this remark must be understood in the context of Kissinger's world view, in which the United Nations played a minor role and a cautious secretary general who would not get in the way of American foreign policy was desirable. Moreover, Waldheim and the United Nations had in 1973–1974 been most valuable to the United States in dealing with the aftermath of the 1973 war between Israel, Egypt, and Syria.

If one looks at the major issues that the United Nations dealt with between 1971 and 1981, two things appear evident. First, except for the important role of U.N. peacekeeping in the Sinai and on the Golan Heights, the United Nations did very little. The major powers generally preferred to deal with important foreign policy issues outside the United Nations. The Third World countries, numbering more than 120, were united in their demands for a New International Economic Order, an end to Apartheid and the "inalienable rights of the Palestinians," but did not have the power to realize those goals against the opposition of those whose concessions would be required. As for the conflicts that were going on, whether civil wars in Cambodia, Ethiopia, the Sudan, Angola, the Western Sahara, Nicaragua, and El Salvador,

or the war between Iran and Iraq, there was always at least one party that wanted to continue the fighting rather than let the United Nations undertake a peacemaking or peacekeeping role. As for the use of force against the party judged responsible for a threat to the peace or a breach of the peace, envisioned in Article 42 of the U.N. charter, that kind of action has never been employed because of political conditions in the world. Such action would require that the five permanent members of the Security Council (Britain, China, France, the Soviet Union, and the United States) agree on the offender and be prepared to use force jointly against that party. In the atmosphere of the Cold War, with the Soviet Union and the United States each perceiving the other as the main threat and each having allies or friends to protect, this has been impossible. The only time force has been used was in Korea, 1950–1953, and that was principally a South Korean–U.S. operation, using a U.N. flag, with fourteen other countries voluntarily contributing contingents. As related earlier, the endorsement of the Security Council was possible only because the Soviets were boycotting the Council in June and July 1950; hence, they were not there to cast the veto.

Second, where the United Nations did play a significant role, United States influence was at least as important as Soviet. The outstanding example was in the 1973 Arab–Israeli war. That conflict began with an Egyptian surprise attack across the Suez Canal on 6 October. The United States immediately requested a meeting of the Security Council. Four meetings were held, without result, between 8 and 12 October. At that stage the Egyptians and Syrians were driving the Israelis back; consequently, the Soviets and Arabs did not want any Security Council action. But the secretary general did report to the Council, on evidence provided by a U.N. team of truce observers (UNTSO), that Egypt had struck first, contrary to the Egyptian version.[8] Nevertheless, supporters of Egypt could argue that it was not the aggressor, since it could claim to be fighting to regain its own territory. And they demanded that, as a cease-fire condition, Israel must withdraw completely from the Sinai and all other territories captured in the 1967 war, including Gaza and the West Bank—a condition clearly unacceptable to Israel and the United States.

By mid-October, Israel, reinforced by a massive airlift of supplies from the United States, was able to turn the tide. Then

Moscow and the Arabs developed an interest in a cease-fire. On 19 October Kissinger flew to Moscow, where negotiations led to a U.S.—Soviet cease-fire plan. On his way back to Washington Kissinger stopped in Israel to brief the government leaders there. The next day the plan was presented to the Security Council without prior consultation. China, in protest, refused to participate in the voting, but the resolution for a cease-fire was passed. Adopted at 10 P.M., the resolution called for a cease-fire in place within twelve hours, and concurrent negotiations under appropriate auspices aimed at establishing a just and durable peace in the Middle East (Security Council Resolution 338, 22 October 1973).

(If Article 27 of the U.N. charter were taken literally, China's nonparticipation would have constituted a veto. That article provides that decisions of the Security Council on all substantive [nonprocedural] matters "shall be made by an affirmative vote of nine members, including the *concurring* votes of the permanent members" [underlining ours]. Literally, absence, abstention or nonvoting could hardly be considered a concurring vote. In practice, however, these have not been treated as vetoes over the entire forty-four years of the United Nations. Only an actual "no" vote has been so considered. Having been accepted by the U.N. Legal Council and, in practice, by the members, this more liberal interpretation of Article 27 has prevailed. It enables a permanent member to disassociate itself from a resolution without blocking it.)

Israeli forces continued their advance, with some elements crossing the Suez Canal and encircling Egypt's Third Army Corps. Alarmed at the prospect of seeing that corps annihilated, President Sadat sent urgent appeals to Washington and Moscow. Brezhnev responded by offering to send in Soviet troops. He proposed to Nixon that the United States and the Soviets both provide forces. Nixon certainly did not want Soviet troops on the Suez Canal; consequently, he put U.S. forces on high alert. A very dangerous Soviet–U.S. confrontation appeared to be brewing.

On 23 October Waldheim called Kissinger to suggest that a U.N. peacekeeping force be interposed between the Egyptian and Israeli forces.[9] Apparently the idea was well-received. The United

States and the Soviets, each for its own reasons, did not want to see the Third Army Corps annihilated. For the Soviets it would mean a further loss of standing in the Arab world, as Arab forces supplied by the Soviets had again been defeated by the U.S.-supplied Israelis. Kissinger, on the other hand, was aware that Sadat was interested in peace negotiations and did not want him so humiliated that it would be impossible for him to negotiate.

On 25 October, at the initiative of Yugoslavia, the Security Council took up the issue of a U.N. peacekeeping force. The United States, determined to exclude the Soviets from participating in any military force, insisted, against Soviet, British, and French opposition, on excluding the forces of permanent members. Supported by the non-aligned members, the U.S. won its point. The secretary general was asked to report within twenty-four hours on the setting up of a force, and the Council accepted his proposals. As Brian Urquhart observes, this ended the risk of armed intervention by the Soviets in Egypt, and the extremely dangerous U.S.–Soviet confrontation was defused.[10] The Soviets were mollified, at Kissinger's suggestion, by the dispatch of thirty-six Soviet observers to join the U.N. truce supervisor organization in the Middle East (UNTSO).

Waldheim was aided by the staff of the undersecretary general for Special Political Affairs, which did a masterful job in preparing a report setting forth the modus vivendi of a peacekeeping force. The Soviets were consulted through Arkady Shevchenko, then undersecretary general for Political and Security Affairs, and agreed that expenses for the force would be borne by the members as assessed by the General Assembly—a provision they had rejected in connection with UNEF I (Middle East) and ONUC (the Congo). They also accepted the appointment of a commander by the secretary general. The United States, on its side, agreed for the first time that "geographic representation" should apply to a peacekeeping force. (A Polish contingent was included and performed to the complete satisfaction of the force commander and the secretary general.) The Soviets insisted that the force be authorized for only six months. The United States, having in mind the abrupt withdrawal of UNEF I at Nasser's request in 1967, put on record Washington's understanding that the force would not

be withdrawn during any period for which it had been authorized by the Council without that body's explicit consent.

UNEF II was reauthorized regularly by the Council. It paved the way for Egypt and Israel to negotiate a series of disengagement agreements, with the help of Kissinger, and thus to build confidence in each other. This mutual confidence, in turn, made possible the Camp David negotiations and the resultant peace treaty. Egypt, Israel, and the United States all wanted UNEF II to monitor observance of the treaty, but Soviet objections made that impossible. Consequently, the United States, in consultation with Egypt and Israel, set up a multinational force outside the U.N. framework. But UNEF II had been of enormous help in progress toward a peace treaty. It had also established a precedent and a framework for future peacekeeping operations.

Waldheim's reaction to the peace treaty was ambivalent. He recognized the treaty "as an important step towards the establishment of peace between two nations" but was concerned about its implications for efforts to achieve a comprehensive settlement that included the Palestinians.[11] His views coincided with those of a majority of members, as expressed in the General Assembly; consequently, they were "safe."

UNEF II also helped pave the way toward the establishment of a buffer force on the Golan Heights. Called UNDOF (U.N. Disengagement Observer Force), it stands between Syrian and Israeli forces and thus provides assurance that neither side will cheat. There have been no clashes on the Golan Heights for fifteen years, not even during Israel's 1982 invasion of Lebanon. Evidently neither Syria nor Israel has wanted a war between them; hence, the area has been quiet. UNDOF has helped to prevent a war by accident.

The United Nations also has a force on Cyprus (UNFICYP) which helped to keep peace between the majority of ethnic Greeks on the island who control the government and the ethnic Turks. UNFICYP was not equipped, however, to fight the sizable army that Turkey landed on Cyprus in 1974. The Turks advanced until they had occupied about a third of the island. The critical point came when the Turkish Army advanced toward the Nicosia International Airport which was held by the National Guard. In order to avoid casualties in this populated area, UNFICYP's commander had

arranged with the local Greek and Turkish commanders for the UNFICYP to take over the airport. Once the National Guard (ethnic Greek) had withdrawn, the Turkish military command announced that it would take over the airport, by force if necessary. Waldheim was visiting Henry Kissinger in Washington on 23 July when George Sherry, the U.N. specialist on Cyprus, called urgently to brief him on the situation. Invited by Kissinger to use American communications facilities, Waldheim phone the Turkish prime minister, Bulent Ecevit, to bring this serious situation, involving potentially a breach of faith, a loss of standing for UNFICYP, and serious bloodshed, to his attention. Ecevit promised to look into the matter. By evening, in response to another call from Waldheim, Ecevit informed him that he had sent the necessary instructions, and the UNFICYP would continue to hold the airport.[12]

In all three of these operations, UNEF II, UNDOF and UNFICYP, Waldheim and his staff appear to have served the interest of international peace as well as the interests of the United States and Israel. Of course, he also catered to the views of the other Members of the United Nations, and there were compromises, but neither the United States nor Israel had reason to be dissatisfied. Nor did the Soviets, the Arabs, the Cypriots, the Greeks, or the Turks.

But the hostage situation in Iran was another story. On 4 November 1979, mobs in Teheran seized the American Embassy and took its diplomatic personnel hostage, in violation of international conventions. Waldheim tried hard to help, immediately sending an appeal to the Ayatollah Khomeini to release the hostages. When there was no response, Waldheim, using his authority under Article 99, on 25 November requested an urgent meeting of the Security Council to consider the situation.[13] The Council adopted a resolution deploring the seizure of hostages and calling on the Iranian government to secure their release. Iran, defiant, refused.

President Carter, deeply disturbed by the continued detention of the hostages, was trying every possible means to secure their release. This included resort not only to the Security Council but also to the International Court of Justice, which also called for release of the hostages. Finally Carter initiated the aborted attempt

to rescue them with American helicopters in April 1980. As part of the overall effort, Donald McHenry, then the U.S. permanent representative, suggested to Waldheim that he go to Teheran personally. Aga Shahi, Pakistan's Foreign Minister, informed Waldheim that he would be received by the Ayatollah Khomeini, but the Iranian Foreign Minister, Sadegh Ghotbzadeh, approached by telephone, refused to confirm it. Nevertheless, Waldheim, prodded by the Americans, decided to go ahead, landing in Iran on New Year's Day. Ghotbzadeh, who had invited Waldheim, met him at the airport but did not appear sanguine about the visit. He urged Waldheim to ''avoid the impression that you are here to negotiate the release of the hostages. The important point to stress is that your visit is a fact-finding mission and not a negotiating mission.''[14]

The media, obviously with official encouragement, were portraying outbursts of anger at the United States, contempt for the West and scorn for the United Nations. The evening television service showed Waldheim's arrival at the airport on a split screen. The other half portrayed victims of brutalities by the Shah's secret police. The next morning's papers showed pictures of Waldheim shaking hands with the Shah during his 1978 visit and others kissing the hand of the Shah's sister, Princess Ashraf. When visiting a cemetary, at the insistence of his hosts, he was chased by a hostile mob and barely made it back to the helicopter. Photographs of him looking scared were criticized but, in the circumstances, he had every reason to be frightened. Carter and Vance were grateful to Waldheim and said so in public but, as Urquhart observed, ''their voices were drowned out by the Iranian mob and the Western media, who seemed delighted to have someone new to blame.''[15]

Though Waldheim made the trip to Teheran partly as a result of an approach by McHenry, who was acting on instructions from Carter and Vance, McHenry alleges that on another occasion the secretary general embarrassed him by lying. In May 1979 Waldheim sent his deputy for African Affairs, Abdelrahim Farah to clear a proposed statement with McHenry on Namibia (Southwest Africa). Subsequently Waldheim altered the statement and, without showing the changes to McHenry, sent it to the government of South Africa with an affirmation that it had been

cleared with McHenry. The South African government reacted angrily and its press denounced McHenry as being biased against South Africa and in favor of SWAPO (the South West Africa People's Organization, a Black guerrilla movement fighting for the independence of Namibia). McHenry called this breach of faith to the attention of Vance, who sent to Waldheim a proposed statement from the secretary general to South Africa making it clear that McHenry had not given his assent. Waldheim refused to send the statement; consequently, the State Department sent the correction. The incident left McHenry with the feeling that Waldheim was not to be trusted. He said that Waldheim would whisper "I'm for you" in order to get along with everybody and tended to bend to pressure. Consequently, McHenry had felt the need to keep the heat on Waldheim when U.S. interests were involved.[16]

McHenry's observation, which was borne out in many other interviews, points to a fundamental weakness of Waldheim as secretary general, that is his tendency to speak and act in a way that would curry favor, rather than out of conviction or a sense of right and wrong. Hammarskjöld had deep convictions and stood up to pressure from governments when he was convinced that his views were in the interest of the United Nations and the implementation of its charter. Waldheim bent with the prevailing winds, trying to please the major powers and the non-aligned. As Brian Urquhart put it, he "seemed to be a man without real substance, quality or character, swept along by an insatiable thirst for public office." Urquhart, who worked closely with Waldheim on major political issues for ten years and is uniquely qualified to observe his performance, describes him as "an energetic, ambitious mediocrity" and as a man who "lacked the qualities of vision, integrity, inspiration and leadership that the United Nations so desperately needs."[17]

The question about Waldheim's role in the area of peace and security cannot be limited to his performance on the Middle East in 1973, Cyprus in 1974, and the hostage crisis in 1980. While it is difficult to fault him on his performance in those three instances, these actions were hardly enough for a decade. The real question is whether other conflicts might have been prevented or stopped by a dynamic secretary general, with a sense of mission, whose diplomatic ability and integrity were widely respected. He

could not have forced governments to settle their conflicts peacefully, but he might have tried to use initiative, imagination and influence to persuade them in that direction. Here we have in mind, for example, conflicts in Southern Africa, the Western Sahara and the Persian Gulf. It is quite possible that the combatants in those areas would have rejected any effort at peaceful settlement during the 1970s and in their particular situations. Perhaps the time was not ripe. Still, one must feel regret that to our knowledge no major effort was made by Waldheim to help resolve these issues.

The Non-Aligned

From the moment of his first candidacy for secretary general in 1971, Waldheim made strenuous efforts to cultivate the non-aligned countries, which constitute a majority of the membership. When asked where his first indications of support came from he said: "The Third World."[18] To them he stressed that he came from a non-aligned country, Austria. He went out of his way to cultivate Marshal Tito; he mentions numerous meetings between them in Belgrade and New York and writes that he was "a frequent guest of his on the two-island complex of Brioni." He reports that two main factors influenced Tito's views on foreign policy: (1) a deep fear of the Soviets, especially after they crushed the "Prague Spring" in 1968 and (2) the strengthening of the structure of the East–West detente and the Non-Aligned Movement. Waldheim describes seeing Tito in Havana during the 1979 summit conference of the Non-Aligned Movement, deeply depressed. Tito was particularly concerned over the election of Cuba to chair the meeting. (By custom, the chair goes to the host country) and by the predominance of the more radical leaders. "He was deeply exercized as to how the Non-Aligned Movement could maintain its credibility if Cuba, with its close links to the Soviet Union, were its leader.[19]

These repeated friendly contacts with Tito are particularly interesting in view of the fact that it was the Yugoslav government that in 1947 brought the charges against Waldheim that constitute the file of the U.N. War Crimes Commission. Moreover, it was

principally against the Yugoslavs that the German army units in the Balkans with which Waldheim served carried out atrocities, including the large-scale murder of civilians. This may indicate either that Tito considered Waldheim to be a very minor cog in the German war machine, or that Tito's fear of the Soviets made the cultivation of Austrian friendship more important than the prosecution of Waldheim, or both.

Waldheim expressed considerable sympathy with the Third World drive for a New International Economic Order, which commanded an overwhelming majority in the General Assembly but got little support from those major industrialized nations whose resources and policy changes would be crucial to the realization of its goals. He deplored the fact that disparities between the rich and poor countries were increasing rather than diminishing and felt that remedial action was necessary. But, as a realist, he observed: "Nothing would be accomplished if the two sides dug in on extreme positions and used the United Nations to launch verbal broadsides at each other. I therefore devoted myself to a search for areas of agreement, the advocacy of moderation and gradualism and the continuation of a dialogue between the parties."[20]

This position recognized the fact that the industrialized countries could not be forced by majority resolutions to provide aid or change policies; they would do so only if persuaded by discussion or by their own analysis that such actions would be in their national interest. Moreover, Waldheim's position enabled him to show sympathy for the Thrid World without offending the major powers, particularly the United States.

The developing countries placed major emphasis on "global negotiations" in the United Nations itself, including issues of aid, trade, finance and monetary issues, and transfer of technologies. The United States and other major industrialized countries strongly preferred to discuss trade issues in the General Agreement on Tariffs and Trade (GATT), where majority voting was not a factor, and development aid and monetary issues in the World Bank (IBRD) and International Monetary Fund (IMF), respectively. In the latter two bodies the representatives were more professional and specialized. Moreover, voting was weighted according to contribution, giving half a dozen industrialized countries a majority of the votes. This continues to be the case.

Despite major efforts by Willi Brandt of West Germany and Pierre Trudeau of Canada, the twain never really met. Differences were papered over by broad generalities, but the New International Economic Order did not see the light of day. It is no longer a major issue, but not because the problems of the developing countries have been solved or ameliorated. On the contrary, with the notable exception of the new Asian "tigers" (South Korea, Taiwan, Singapore and Hong Kong), most of the developing countries have failed to grow significantly in the 1980s and many have witnessed a decline, particularly in Africa. The foreign debt of many of them has become so massive that it now constitutes the core of negotiations with the industrialized countries. This emergency has become absorbing, and the idea of global negotiations on a New International Economic Order has receded into the background.

Returning to the matter of Waldheim's cultivation of the Non-Aligned Movement (NAM), the following observation by Thomas Franck is pertinent.

> Secretaries-General are not naive, but they are politically attuned. Ever since Dag Hammarskjöld learned to lean on the NAMs for support in the face of Soviet attacks on his policies in the Congo, incumbents have frequently linked the neutrality of their office with the cold-war neutralism of the NAMs. At times, usually in private, they do encourage the NAMs to modify their more extreme positions on such issues as the demand for economic concessions from the industrialized nations and on sanctions against Israel. But these are exceptional demonstrations of the traditional independence of the office. During the Cuban missile crisis as well as in the Vietnam War, U Thant relied upon the support of the NAMs in staking out the Secretary-General's position and giving it the weight of "world conscience." As this reliance has increased, the office has ceased to be solely the "conscience of the world" and has seemed to become, at times, the "conscience" of India, Algeria, Nigeria, and Mexico.[21]

Refugees Relief and Human Rights

One area in which Waldheim worked with energy and effectiveness was in assistance to refugees. In the wake of the war in Bangla Desh in 1971, the new government was faced with massive devastation, dislocation of people, and starvation. Deeply touched by what he saw when visiting there, Waldheim consulted Sadruddin Aga Khan, the high commissioner for refugees, and his own deputy, Brian Urquhart. He then appointed Sir Robert Jackson, who had distinguished himself in many U.N. operations, to take charge of relief and resettlement operations in Bangla Desh. With generous responses from governments, the operation was a resounding success. Soviet teams cleared the major port, Chittagong, while Americans carried out reconstruction work in the capital, Dacca, and other parts of the country. Several European countries and international relief agencies also helped, and the work was completed in a relatively short time.[22]

Waldheim also used his personal initiative and influence to mount a campaign to help the "boat people," predominantly ethnic Chinese fleeing Vietnam after Ho Chi Minh's conquest of South Vietnam. Many were shipwrecked or robbed and killed by pirates. Often passing vessels refused to rescue the refugees, because the countries where the ships were registered would not accept them. Moreover, Thailand and other countries of first asylum were being swamped with refugees and were anxious that these homeless people be resettled.

Shortly after her election, Prime Minister Margaret Thatcher sent Waldheim a personal message urging him to take action. Waldheim first replied that, since the Economic and Social Council was not in session, he was not authorized to take an initiative under the U.N. charter and rules and procedures of the Economic and Social Council. Subsequently, after consulting other governments, including those of the Soviet bloc, who raised no objections, Waldheim convened in Geneva, in cooperation with the U.N. high commissioner for refugees, a high-level meeting with representatives of those countries willing to take part. Over the course of two days, offers of resettlement doubled from 125,000 to 260,000. Substantial new pledges of assistance in cash or in kind were made, totalling more that $160 million. Thailand,

Malaysia, and Indonesia agreed to stop expelling refugees. The United States doubled its monthly quota for receiving refugees from Indo-China and sent rescue ships to the South China Sea. Subsequently, Waldheim worked out an agreement with the Vietnamese authorities to reduce the exodus.[23]

In terms of numbers, an even more serious problem developed in Africa. In January 1972 there were approximately three-quarters of a million refugees in Africa, largely victims of civil war and ethnic strife. By 1981 there were more than five million in eighteen different countries. On Waldheim's recommendation the General Assembly authorized a conference in Geneva to consider the problem. The conference was attended by representatives of ninety-nine governments, who pledged over $550 million to help expand relief operations.[24]

Blocked in his Assembly-mandated efforts to negotiate Vietnamese withdrawal from Kampuchea, the secretary general, acting entirely on his own, organized a highly successful pledging conference to fund a gigantic relief effort on behalf of Kampuchean refugees. Singapore's respected U.N. ambassador, T. T. B. Koh, has said that "if the Cambodian nation has survived, it is due in no small part to the humanitarian relief operation started by Secretary-General Waldheim."[25]

Waldheim's actions on behalf of these refugees are in marked contrast to his inaction when Austrian and Greek Jews were being sent to death camps. The circumstances, however, were also markedly different. Opposing the Nazis would have involved serious personal risk, and, as he said when interviewed, he was no hero. As secretary general he had significant prestige and status, could expect recognition for his work on behalf of the refugees, and took no personal risk.

Meanwhile, the U.N. high commissioner for refugees, who has responsibility for refugee programs all around the world, has continued to carry out substantial refugee programs in Africa and Central America and to assist more than three million Afghan refugees in Pakistan and Iran.

In the area of human rights, Waldheim recognized the conflict between Article 2(7) of the U.N. charter, which rules out intervention "in matters which are essentially within the domestic jurisdiction of any state," and the principles of human rights embodied

in the charter. He took the position that this conflict should be resolved in favor of the secretary general's right to intervene whenever the problem reaches the threshold of world conscience. He asserted this right with respect to Vietnamese boat people, as noted above, and to Ethiopean and Chilean political prisoners.[26] (Like his predecessors, he found no difficulty in criticizing Apartheid and other major violations of human rights in South Africa, which have been condemned consistently by the General Assembly and by virtually all governments.)

The problem with this criterion is the difficulty in determining "the threshold of world conscience." Thus Waldheim has been severely criticized for his failure to condemn massive killings in Burundi, by Idi Amin in Uganda and by the Khmer Rouge in Cambodia, and for ignoring egregious violations of human rights in Iran, the Soviet Union, and China.[27]

Waldheim was himself aware of the limitations of his efforts and that he had dealt with only a tiny fraction of human rights violations around the world. He writes: "I am very much aware—much to my regret—that our efforts merely scratched the surface, while the rule of injustice and terror still holds sway" and describes repeated disappointment concerning the upholding of human rights.[28]

Chapter 5

The Secretariat: Personnel, Budget, and Finance

The politicization and consequent deterioration of the Secretariat staff had begun before Waldheim became secretary general. He accelerated the politicization and the deterioration in ways that were damaging to both its morale and performance.[1]

A major contributing factor has been the increasing pressure by governments to get jobs for their nationals. Under the original concept of an international civil service some 75 percent of all the posts were held by career people with lifelong tenure. As the organization grew from its original 51 members to 156 by the time Waldheim left the job, the new members began to clamor in the General Assembly for a greater share of the Secretariat jobs. A large number of posts continued to be held by career civil servants who had entered young in the U.N.'s early years. Thus, original members like France, Britain, the United States, the Philippines, Egypt, and India tended to have a larger number of professional posts, either at the top of their "desirable range" or above it. Newer members, even developed countries like Japan and the Federal Republic of Germany, tended to be below their "desirable range." The Soviet Union, though an original member, has been below its "desirable range" mainly because it has insisted on a fixed-term rather than career appointments for its nationals. With a persistent turnover of Soviets in the Secretariat

every two or three years, it was difficult both to recruit new people as replacements and also increase the number of posts held by the Soviets.

The "desirable range" is a target the organization uses in projecting its recruitment needs. It is calculated by allowing a certain minimum of posts (2 to 7) to each member state, then distributing 200 posts among the regions to reflect population distribution, and finally allocating the remaining posts among members according to their contributions to the U.N.'s regular budget. Thus, the United States, which is assessed 25 percent of the budget, has the highest desirable range (327-442) and the Soviets about half the U.S. figure. Japan follows closely behind, as its national income and its assessment in the U.N. budget have increased markedly.

With respect to personnel, Article 101, paragraph 3 of the U.N. charter stipulates: "The paramount consideration in the employment of the staff and in the determination of conditions of service shall be the necessity of securing the highest standards of efficiency, competence and integrity. Due regard shall be paid to the importance of recruiting the staff on as wide a geographical basis as possible."

The new members, principally from Africa, Asia, and the Caribbean have emphasized, in General Assembly discussions of budget and personnel, the importance of geographical distribution. Since many of them are below the desirable range in Secretariat staffing, they want to put pressure on the secretary general to give preference to their nationals in filling posts. They are backed by the Soviets who, because of their doctrine of letting their nationals take only fixed-term rather than career assignments, have been chronically under their desirable range. The result has been a series of annual General Assembly resolutions instructing the secretary general to make special efforts to recruit nationals of countries below their desirable range.

George Davidson, a Canadian who served as undersecretary general for Administration under Waldheim, 1972-1979, states: "The principle of 'equitable geographical distribution' laid down by the Charter was progressively interpreted to mean 'equitable national distribution,' to the point where today the Personnel Division of the U.N. is, in effect, required to give priority to this

formula in carrying out its activities—relegating such factors as experience, competence and integrity, to secondary consideration."[2]

Davidson goes on to assert that the shift in emphasis was dictated by the General Assembly, not by the secretary general, who was obliged to carry out the Assembly's mandates. This is not to say that persons of competence and integrity cannot be found in the new countries. Many of their people have done an excellent job in the Secretariat. But the emphasis on nationality and desirable range has tended to weaken the stress on competence.

The pressure of the Assembly resolutions was followed up by pressures from individual members to get jobs for their nationals. Sometimes this was occasioned by government policy, with the thought that jobs could provide influence on Secretariat operations. In other cases, the motive was cronyism; a permanent representative or a member of the Mission staff wanted to help a friend or relative. For the Soviets, the motives are influence on Secretariat operations, opportunities to gain dollars (Soviet nationals are obliged to turn over a portion of their salaries), and opportunities for espionage.[3]

As for Waldheim, the question is whether he tried to interpret the resolutions in terms of the charter's emphasis on competence, resisting undue politicization. The answer is that he did not. When he was importuned by government representatives for jobs, he could have said that he did not deal with such matters. Such was U Thant's approach, in general. Waldheim, by contrast, did discuss jobs and tended to use them as a way of ingratiating himself with governments, like a politician building support through patronage. During his tenure of ten years, the number of senior posts increased by 25 percent. As mentioned earlier, Soviet Ambassador Malik would tell Waldheim bluntly that, unless the Soviet Union got certain jobs, he would not be reelected secretary general.

Waldheim drew criticism from the United States when he signed on to the appointment of Geli Dneprovsky for the post of director of personnel at the U.N.'s European headquarters. The United States lodged a strong complaint, on the grounds that Dneprovsky was a KGB official and should not be in a position of supervising the records of over 3,000 U.N. employees in Geneva. Waldheim and Davidson asked the United States for

evidence and, when none was produced, went ahead with the appointment. Waldheim writes: "He had served perfectly well in New York, and as the accusations were not pressed and no evidence was presented, the affair blew over."[4] On the other hand, Shevchenko identifies Dneprovsky as a veteran KGB recruiter "who became the mastermind of U.N. operations during three New York tours from 1965 to 1978." Shevchenko refers to the Geneva job as "an *equally* strategic personnel post."[5] (Underlining ours). This may explain why the United States did not press the issue.

Waldheim's relations with Secretariat staff left much to be desired. His interference in appointments, even at lower levels, for reasons of political patronage caused resentment among those who were not so favored. He was polite, even obsequious, toward government representatives but cold and arrogant toward ordinary staff.[6]

Theodore Kheel, a veteran and respected mediator, agreed to represent the U.N. staff, for a nominal fee, in its struggle with the administration. He reports that, in forty years of labor mediation, he never encountered anything approaching the U.N.'s authoritarian attitude toward staff. He observes: "Waldheim would be a better international mediator if he'd eschew the role of ayatolla toward his own staff." According to Kheel, "The thing that utterly amazed me was the position taken by the Secretary-General of the United Nations to disregard the elementary established rights of the employees: that the agency created to maintain standards of human decency and to bring about peace by negotiated settlement would violate its own agreements and see no necessity for compliance with its own word."[7]

Waldheim has also been faulted for his failure to defend U.N. Secretariat employees illegally imprisoned by governments. A notable case involved Alicja Weselowska, a young Polish member of the U.N. staff, who was arrested by Polish authorities in Warsaw while she was en route to a U.N. assignment in Mongolia. Convicted on a charge of "contacts with foreign intelligence," for which no evidence was produced, she was sentenced to seven years in prison and actually served five. This was in violation of United Nations conventions, to which Poland is a signatory, regarding the rights and immunities of international

civil servants—essential to the standing and safety of every U.N. employee. Yet Waldheim was reluctant to press the Polish government. He was finally induced to make an appeal to Polish authorities only by insistent staff protests and by public pressure as the story was aired in the Western press.[8]

On the other hand, our extensive interviews revealed no evidence of overt anti-Semitism on Waldheim's part. These included many Jewish staff members. This evaluation was also shared by David Popper, who helped to write the first draft of Waldheim's book, *In the Eye of the Storm*, and Jeane Kirkpatrick, who was U.S. permanent representative when Waldheim was secretary general.[9]

Indeed, he appeared to go out of his way to cultivate American Jews. His last three books were written with the help of two American and one French Jew: Popper, mentioned above, Robert Schiffer, who edited *Building the Future Order*, and Eric Rouleau, who drafted *Un Metier Unique au Monde*. We have already referred to his friendly relationship with Lord Weidenfeld, publisher of his last book. His lawyer and doctor in New York were both Jewish.

Also on the positive side is Waldheim's selection of his top deputies. George Davidson, his undersecretary general for Administration, was knowledgeable about the United Nations, and had held two ministerial posts in the Canadian Government. He had been president of the Canadian Broadcasting Corporation when he was appointed by Waldheim. Brian Urquhart, his principal political deputy, was a most competent and experienced officer, a true heir to Ralph Bunche. Jean Ripert, a Frenchman, had excellent economic credentials and was thoroughly familiar with the U.N. when Waldheim named him undersecretary general for Economic and Social Affairs. Roberto Guyer, an experienced Argentine diplomat, was eminently qualified to be undersecretary general for Special Political Affairs and, in that capacity, to undertake diplomatic missions for the secretary general. Eric Suy, a Belgian, performed very competently as legal counsel. Waldheim was also well-served in the post of undersecretary general for General Assembly Affairs by Bradford Morse who resigned from the U.S. Congress to take the post, and by William Buffum, a career American diplomat with extensive U.N. experience, who

succeeded Morse. These top deputies, along with his inner cabinet of Austrians, were selections in which a secretary general should be personally involved, and Waldheim used good judgement in choosing them. His mistake was in intervening further down the line in the Secretariat for his own political purposes.

Another weakness was in the areas of administration and finance. He had little interest in or understanding of these areas. George Saddler relates how he would provide Waldheim with a statement on program budgeting and explain it carefully, but it appeared to roll right off the secretary general's back.[10] On the other hand, Waldheim did call for fiscal restraint (probably to please the major contributors, like the United States, the USSR, Japan, and the Western Europeans). He urged a redeployment of resources and a rearrangement of priorities so that new activities would be financed out of the resources released as a result of the completion or discontinuation of old activities. He also urged that there be fewer meetings or conferences.[11]

Unfortunately, the Assembly majority, which paid for only a tiny portion of the budget, paid little heed to Waldheim's exhortations and went on voting increased budgets, despite the rising opposition of the major contributors.

Waldheim did not apply any concern with economy to his personal perquisites. He love pomp and ceremony. He furnished the secretary general's residence, donated to the United Nations by Arthur A. Houghton, Jr., with expensive furniture, Saxe porcelain, fine silver, and lavish gifts from heads of state; for example, an antique clock from the President of Mexico and a rug from the King of Saudi Arabia. There were also diamonds from the Shah of Iran, which Waldheim reportedly kept for himself.[12] He envied ministers and presidents who had private planes but was never able to have one as secretary general.

Perhaps Waldheim's biggest frustration, other than failing to win a third term as secretary general, was his inability to woo the media successfully. He paid great attention to his public image and was always ready to talk to reporters. He would have liked to get the kind of coverage accorded to Henry Kissinger. Unfortunately for Waldheim, the United Nations was making little positive, sensational news during his tenure; governments were choosing to deal elsewhere with their major security problems.

There were two major exceptions, the aftermath of the 1973 Arab-Israeli war, when the United Nations had a most important role in defusing a potentially dangerous Soviet–U.S. confrontation in the Middle East, and Waldheim's trip to Teheran in 1980 in a vain effort to assist in the release of the American hostages there. In the latter case, unfortunately, the media stressed his fear when he was surrounded by a menacing Iranian mob rather than the fact that he had undertaken a difficult and dangerous mission in response to a plea from President Carter.

The other reason for Waldheim's frustration was personal. In general, reporters did not find him interesting to interview. His manner was stiff and his articulation anything but lively. There were few quotable statements and precious little humor. Brian Urquhart observes:

Waldheim worried a great deal about his public image, but his efforts to tackle this problem usually made things worse. He was too anxious to be given credit and tended to be too accessible to the media. He frequently had to resort to cliches and to bland, noncommittal statements which bored the press. His manner sometimes seemed ingratiating, and he tried too hard with too little to say. Indeed, the discretion imposed upon the Secretary-General by his position as honest broker between governments greatly limits his capacity to interest the media. All in all Waldheim had an unfortunate public personality.

Waldheim tended to make off-the-cuff statements and later to try to retract or alter them. He spent hours editing the transcripts of press conferences he had already given. He occasionally lost his temper with journalists, with disastrous results. He was acutely sensitive to negative press reports, of which the United Nations routinely suffers a great many, and his efforts to deal with them usually made matters worse.[13]

Chapter 6

The Third Try

Given his lackluster performance, it may seem surprising that he would have won a third five-year term as secretary general in 1981, had there not been a persistent Chinese veto of him. Even the Chinese position appears to have been based on a desire to show solidarity with the Third World rather than a grievance against Waldheim.

How could this be? It appears that the Reagan Administration, Brezhnev, Thatcher, and the French government were content to have a plodding bureaucrat who would not take initiatives that might disturb them. They did not expect the United Nations to serve their major foreign policy objectives; they just did not want it to get in their way.

There was also the question of alternatives. Since Europe had provided three secretaries general, covering 24 of the 36 years of the United Nations' existence, there was a strong feeling among the Third World countries that it was their turn. Asia had had one, U Thant of Burma, for ten years. Why not have a new secretary general from Africa or Latin America?

The leading African candidate, Salim Salim, was anethema to the United States. He had been the principal antagonist during the 1971 debate over Chinese representation, and allegedly danced in the aisle to celebrate the defeat of the American two-China

proposal or, in any event, was prominent in the celebration. Moreover, he represented a leftist Socialist regime (Tanzania). There was no way the United States would accept him. Washington could be comfortable with Waldheim who had done nothing upsetting to the U.S. during his ten-year tenure. Certainly the new Reagan Administration, which had little faith in any international institution, was not looking for a secretary general who would stretch his authority to the limit. There was no doubt about American support for Waldheim, and this was clearly expressed by the U.S. permanent representative, Jeane Kirkpatrick, Vice President George Bush, and Secretary of State Haig.[1] There had been rumblings about Waldheim's wartime record, in letters from constituents to Congressman Stephen Solarz and an article in the *New Republic*. Solarz wrote the secretary general in November 1980, enclosing the letters from his constituents and the *New Republic* article, but Waldheim emphatically denied the charges.[2] Even though Washington had the UNWCC list, including Waldheim's name, it made no move to examine the files that were readily available to it.

The Soviets, too, had made it clear that they would back Waldheim because, as Ambassador Troyanovsky put it, "an old shoe fits better than a new one."[3] The British and French also voted for Waldheim.

In the first ballot late in October 1981 both Salim and Waldheim received more than the necessary nine votes, but each was vetoed—Salim by the U.S. and Waldheim by China. By the third ballot Salim's tally fell to six; France, Spain, and Ireland, which had voted for both Salim and Waldheim in the first ballot, had dropped their support for Salim. But China maintained its veto of Waldheim.

The deadlock continued into December. Then, according to Waldheim, the Chinese indicated to him that they would accept a splitting of the forthcoming term between him and Salim, with each to serve two and a half years. This idea was rejected. Ambassador Kirkpatrick said: "How can we accept Salim for two and a half years, since he is on no account acceptable to us for a full term? That would not be logical."[4] As for China, Waldheim relates: "The Chinese assured me that there was nothing personal in their position, that they appreciated our past fruitful

cooperation, but that after three Europeans had been Secretary-General they believed it was now necessary for a representative of the Third World to assume the post."[5]

Two things are worthy of comment here. First, Waldheim gives no indication that he would have rejected the split term if the United States had agreed to it. Second, despite his lackluster performance in his ten years as secretary-general, none of the permanent members expressed dissatisfaction with him. It appears that, in the context of world politics of that era, with the major powers more concerned that a secretary general might create problems for them than that he might be too cautious, a tireless, careful bureaucrat like Waldheim was quite acceptable. Moreover, the fact that Waldheim consistently polled more than nine votes in the Security Council indicates that he was also acceptable to other members, not just the major powers. Israel, not a member of the Council, considered Waldheim, "the least unacceptable."[6]

Meanwhile other Third World candidates had been waiting in the wings, including Ambassador Carlos Ortiz de Rosas of Argentina, Prince Sadruddin Aga Khan, and Sridath Ramphal, the secretary general of the Commonwealth. All three of these had been candidates in 1971 when the Soviets had rejected Ortiz de Rosas and Sadruddin. Apparently such objectives surfaced again when the president of the Security Council conducted a straw poll. When the Council met for its next ballot, Javier Perez de Cuellar of Peru was elected. He met the Chinese requirement that the new secretary general be from the Third World. The Soviets had known him as Peru's ambassador to Moscow and as Waldheim's special representative for Afghanistan and apparently found him acceptable. Britain, France, and the United States also supported him.

Of the new secretary general, Brian Urquhart observes:

> I had known Perez de Cuellar well for many years. After a time as Peruvian Ambassador to the U.N., he had spent two years as our Special Representative in Cyprus and had then become my opposite number as Under Secretary-General for Special Political Affairs. He was well qualified by experience and ability—a quiet, highly intelligent, and

civilized man with a wide knowledge of the job he was undertaking. Whether he was *too* civilized, or too lacking in ego or cutting edge, remained to be seen. The fact was that out of an apparently hopeless situation, a reasonable and qualified Secretary-General had emerged.[7]

We ourselves had occasion to get acquainted with Perez de Cuellar, notably in urging him to do whatever was feasible to prevent or restrain obnoxious anti-Semitic statements by delegates to the General Assembly. We found him to be thoroughly sympathetic and a man of noteworthy decency. In 1988, patient work by Perez de Cuellar and his deputies, and the conjuncture of world events, led to a series of successes that gave new life to the United Nations. Agreements were brokered for the Soviet Union to withdraw its forces from Afghanistan and for a ceasefire between Iran and Iraq. Moreover, there were promising signs of a peaceful resolution of conflicts in the Western Sahara, Angola, and Namibia (South West Africa). Indeed, in 1989, agreement was reached on measures designed to lead to the independence of Namibia from South Africa and the gradual withdrawal of Cuban troops from Angola. Meanwhile under Gorbachev, the Soviets, who had hitherto been against an active and effective role for the secretary general, had begun to call for a revitalized United Nations, which necessarily involves a more active role for the secretary general. The Soviets have paid the United Nations 200 million dollars in arrears, urged a strengthening of U.N. peacekeeping—for which the United Nations received a Nobel Peace Prize in 1988—and called for increased international cooperation through the United Nations in dealing with political, economic, ecological, and humanitarian problems.[8]

As for Waldheim, he was offered and accepted a post at Georgetown University as research professor of diplomacy and counsellor for its Landegger program on business diplomacy; the latter program was endowed by Karl Landegger, an Austrian who had become a highly successful industrialist in the United States. Waldheim had been friendly with Landegger in New York. Waldheim was not required to give regular lectures but rather to direct special seminars on international affairs. It also gave him the opportunity during a two-year stay in Washington, D.C. to

organize his voluminous personal files and write his memoirs, with the help of David Popper and a research team. Popper, a retired American foreign service officer, wrote most of the first draft of the memoirs, which emerged as the book, *In the Eye of the Storm*.

In 1983, after almost seventeen years of residence in the United States, Waldheim went home to Vienna. Three years later he was elected president of Austria. It was in all likelihood his campaign for the presidency that prompted his political opponents to provide to *Profil*, a Viennese journal, an account of Waldheim's service in the Balkans with German army units that committed war crimes—as we have recounted in chapter 1. Otherwise the subject might have remained buried. The *Profil* article triggered an investigation by the World Jewish Congress, which revealed details of his Balkan service and called worldwide attention to the charges against Waldheim. He became a victim of his insatiable ambition.

Chapter 7

The United Nations and the Secretary General in a Changing World

Kurt Waldheim's performance as secretary general might best be described as uneven and unspectacular.

On the positive side, he worked extremely hard and picked well-qualified people for his top deputies. His confidence in Roberto Guyer, Brian Urquhart, and Javier Perez de Cuellar and their associates in the Office of Special Political Affairs was well-placed. He did not deviate significantly from the advice of these experienced professionals. Moreover, he used good judgement in the choice of his other top deputies. He also showed compassion and helped to mount relief programs for refugees in Bangla Desh, Southeast Asia, and Africa. There appears to be no evidence of bias against the United States or Israel, nor in favor of the Soviets.

On the other hand, Waldheim's relations with staff below the level of assistant secretary general were marred by his arrogance toward them. Moreover, his intervention in the appointment and promotion procedures in order to grant political favors accelerated the decline in the quality and morale of the Secretariat. Although he urged budgetary restraint on the General Assembly he had little expertise in budget and finance. He did not understand program budgeting and, during his tenure the number of high-level posts increased by 25 percent.

Though Waldheim devoted much time and energy to cultivating the political leaders of member states and made a special effort with the major powers, he did not gain much respect or trust. He carried his desire to please to the point of being obsequious, and it made him vulnerable to pressure.

Perhaps his most important shortcoming was that he failed to win the respect of major government leaders, like Nixon, Kissinger, and Gromyko. These leaders were not inclined in the 1970s to attach much importance to the United Nations anyway, and their low opinion of Waldheim may have made them even less inclined to do so. Similarly, he failed to win the respect of the media. Though he wooed media representatives assiduously, they did not find him interesting, a situation which did not help the image of the United Nations. He did not offer inspiring leadership, if it could be called leadership at all. He did not have the dedication to ideals, principles, or moral integrity to move governments beyond their narrow, short-term self-interest. These are the main potential assets of a secretary general, to inspire and persuade United Nations members to use their power and authority on behalf of the common goals of the United Nations charter—peace, justice, human rights, and a livable world. Instead Waldheim was a mere broker among governments on the rare occasions when they chose to enlist his services.

Nevertheless, Waldheim's performance was evidently satisfactory to the four permanent members who voted in 1981 to give him a third five-year term. Even China which vetoed his election in 1981, did not express dissatisfaction with Waldheim personally; it was prepared to accept a compromise under which he would share a split term.[1]

But we have seen that these governments, in the period 1971-1981, did not consider the United Nations to be a major factor in international relations, nor did they want it to be; hence, the selection of the best qualified candidate for secretary general did not have a high priority for them. For the Soviets, the main concern was not to have another Hammarskjöld, whose dynamism and independence prompted actions they conceived to be against Soviet national interests. In this situation an ambitious, hard-working bureaucrat like Waldheim coming from neutral Austria, appeared to be safe. Moreover, in the context of

the Cold War, there was a tendency among major governments (and even Yugoslavia) to overlook or not inquire very diligently into the activities of Germans and Austrians during World War II if they were perceived to be useful in the new context.[2] It was not an abstraction called the United Nations that enabled Waldheim to be elected and reelected secretary general. It was the member states, especially the major powers.

Now, however, there is a new situation. For four decades the Soviets showed little interest in an effective United Nations and used it mainly for propaganda. Now, under President Mikhail Gorbachev, they appear to regard it as potentially a very important instrument for maintaining international peace and security. In his much publicized 1987 article, "Realities and Guarantees for a Secure World," Gorbachev proposes the establishment of a system of international peace and security that "could function on the basis of the U.N. Charter and within the framework of the United Nations." He supports the proposal of the secretary general "to set up under the United Nations Organization a multilateral center for lessening the danger of war." He suggests considering "the expediency of setting up a direct communication line between the United Nations headquarters and the capitals of the countries that are permanent members of the Security Council, and the location of the chairman of the non-aligned movement"—a kind of multilateral hotline. He proposes the establishment, under the aegis of the United Nations, of a mechanism "for extensive international verification of compliance with agreements on lessening international tension and limiting armaments. The mechanism would use various forms and methods of monitoring to collect information and submit it to the United Nations. This would provide an objective picture of the events taking place and timely detection of preparations for hostilities, impede sneak attacks, make possible measures to avert any armed conflict, and prevent such conflicts from expanding and becoming worse." He continues: "We are arriving at the conclusion that wider use should be made of United Nations military observers and United Nations peace-keeping forces for disengaging the troops of warring sides and for ensuring that ceasefire and armistice agreements are observed."[3]

Gorbachev's support for U.N. peacekeeping operations is all the more noteworthy in view of the fact that for more than thirty years the Soviets denied the legitimacy of U.N. peacekeeping forces and refused to pay their share of such operations, until the establishment of UNEF II and UNDOF in 1973. And his words have been followed by action; in 1988, the Soviets paid over $200 million arrears. (Meanwhile, the United States, which until 1981 had always paid its assessments, has run up arrears of over $400 million.) In his 1987 article, Gorbachev also advocates ''a drastic intensification and expansion of cooperation between states in uprooting international terrorism . . . within the framework of the United Nations.''[4]

The functions Gorbachev endorses imply the need for an effective secretary general. Indeed, Gorbachev states specifically: ''The international community elects an authoritative figure enjoying everybody's trust to that high post. Since the Secretary General is functioning as a representative of every member-country of the organization, all states should give him the maximum of support and help him in fulfilling his responsible mission. The international community should encourage the United Nations Secretary General in his missions of good offices, mediation and reconciliation.''[5]

In October 1988, Vladimir Petrovsky, deputy minister of foreign affairs of the USSR, expanded on Gorbachev's ideas. He declared to the U.N. General Assembly: ''The Soviet Union stands for an ever greater role of the U.N. Secretary-General in solving questions of maintaining international peace and security. The Secretary-General could request the convening of the Security Council, inform the Council on a regular basis on the developments of conflict areas or on other matters, and submit, *on his own initiative*, reports on matters regarding the maintenance of international peace and security, including disarmament. In our view, there is a need to introduce a regular practice of thorough consideration by General Assembly sessions of annual reports of the Secretary General on the work of the Organization and the adoption, if necessary, of decisions on the conclusions and recommendations contained therein'' (emphasis added).[6]

These statements by Petrovsky and Gorbachev represent a dramatic reversal of the Soviet position over many decades that

the secretary general should limit his activities to administration and to carrying out the instructions of the Security Council, the General Assembly, the Economic and Social Council, and the Trusteeship Council, as specified in Articles 97 and 98 of the Charters. Petrovsky's statement came during a year in which U.N. peacekeeping forces were awarded the Nobel Peace Prize. It was also a year in which, following patient, skillful diplomacy by Secretary General Perez de Cuellar and his representatives, agreement was reached on a cease-fire between Iran and Iraq and on a withdrawal of Soviet forces from Afghanistan. In 1989 came an agreement on independence for Namibia (Southwest Africa), with the help of U.N. good offices and peacekeeping, and the gradual withdrawal of Cuban troops from Angola. There were also promising signs of a peaceful settlement of the armed conflict in the Western Sahara, between Morocco and the Polisario.

It is clear, of course, that agreements were possible only when the parties were ready to agree. The United Nations was not in a position to use coercion. But in all of these instances the parties found the United Nations, particularly the office of the secretary general, to be a valuable instrument. It offered good offices, mediation and, where required, military observers and peacekeeping forces to bolster mutual confidence that a cease-fire or armistice would be respected.

Oran Young has pointed out that the secretary general and the Secretariat may be better situated than most third parties to play the role of intervenor in terms of such factors as (1) impartiality between the principal parties, (2) salience in the eyes of the protagonists, (3) prestige and respect accorded to suggestions, (4) ability to act coherently, and (5) availability of diplomatic skill.[7] Clearly the willingness of countries party to a dispute or conflict to seek the secretary general's help in resolving it will depend significantly on the amount of confidence they have in the office holder. And, in the absence of a skilled, trusted mediator, conflicts may be prolonged unnecessarily.

The United Nations can be valuable not only in mediation but also as a face-saver. It is quite possible that the Soviets would have decided to withdraw their forces from Afghanistan even without the good offices of the secretary general. But the cover of an agreement under U.N. auspices helped to save face.

Similar face-saving efforts by the secretary general facilitated the Dutch withdrawal from West Irian in 1963 and the Shah's willingness to give up his claim to Bahrein.[8] And during the Cuban missile crisis, the secretary general's appeal to Krushchev and Kennedy for patience and restraint helped to gain time for Moscow and Washington to work out a peaceful solution.[9]

To a substantial extent the "epidemic of peace" in 1988 and 1989, with the United Nations and its secretary general having a significant role, may be traced to a drastic change of the Soviet position on the role of the United Nations and its secretary general. This development gives rise to three questions. First, why now? Second, will the current Soviet view continue even after Gorbachev or will the USSR revert to its former position? Third, what are the implications for the United Nations and world peace?

On the first, Soviet actions as well as statements in the Gorbachev era appear to indicate a number of policies congruent with a more effective United Nations. The treaty on the elimination of medium-range weapons from Europe, progress toward a convention on the elimination of chemical weapons, and a projected treaty aimed at reducing strategic nuclear weapons by 50 percent, all point toward a lessening emphasis on the use of force and, consequently, greater emphasis on the reduction of tensions and the peaceful settlement of disputes as envisaged in the U.N. charter. Moreover, the USSR has demonstrated a greater interest in the peaceful settlement of "regional" disputes; that is, disputes in and among Third World countries, many of which have involved the USSR and/or the United States directly or indirectly. Without a change in the Soviet position, there would have been no agreement on withdrawal of troops from Afghanistan, and there would have been greater problems in the agreement on Namibian independence and the withdrawal of Cuban troops from Angola.

Why have the Soviets changed their positions on these issues? Here one must speculate, since motives are often very difficult to determine in foreign relations. Gorbachev has embarked on an ambitious program of Perestroika (restructuring the Soviet economy). That program will clearly be helped if tensions with the West can be lessened and the arms burden reduced. The Soviet Union needs at least part of its capital and other resources

devoted to armaments for restructuring and reinvigorating its economy. It also needs advanced technology and some capital, in the form of investments and credits, from the West. Consequently, a foreign policy that is less aggressive and less threatening to the West will help Perestroika, and the United Nations is a handy instrument to pursue such a policy.

We (specifically Saltzman) had meetings with members of the Politburo, namely, Gorbachev, Shevardnadze, Niskinov and a number of members of the Central Committee (numerous meetings from 1985 to 1989). They spoke very frankly to Saltzman, since they were desirous of having their views transmitted to the United States. Gorbachev was concerned, in 1985, that the Soviet Union was falling behind technologically and industrially and would enter the twenty-first century far behind countries such as West Germany, Japan, and the United States. He was also concerned that a generation was growing up not hardened to sacrifice by (a) the Revolution and (b) the Great War, and were seeking an improved standard of living, particularly consumer goods. These pressures were pushing the Soviet Union towards arms reduction, which meant greater accommodation with the United States and less tension throughout the world. It also meant that they recognized the need to come closer to Western economic institutions such as the International Monetary Fund (IMF), the World Bank, and the General Agreement on Tariffs and Trade (GATT). Further, it meant that the economic rigidities of doctrine and Marxism would increasingly give place to "market place" economic solutions and that the Soviet Union would in due course be part of the world economic system. This approach to rapprochement with the West caused an increasing desire on the part of the Soviet Union to work more closely with the United Nations, itself a vehicle for wide-ranging international arrangements.

This internal revolution which has intensified, was expressed to Saltzman in May of 1987 by the spokesman for the Central Committee of the USSR in a startling exchange:

> *Question from Saltzman*: These broad economic changes, including free market economic techniques are radical departures from Soviet economic thinking and how do you equate them with Leninism?

Answer: Lenin would have advocated whatever he felt was in the interests of the Soviet people and this new approach would have had his approval.

Question by Saltzman: If the economy is liberalized to this extent, will it not follow that political liberalism will inevitably take hold?

Answer: There is no turning back. There is no other way.

The fundamental changes in the Soviet Union caused by economic factors that leaders in the Soviet Union are realistic enough to recognize and accept will find their reflection in new political approaches throughout the world; thus, the Soviet Union has also taken a different posture in the United Nations and has shown a disposition to function within the United Nations as part of its global reappraisal.

On the second question, the answer must also be somewhat speculative. A Soviet government that has reversed its negative attitude toward the United Nations could, of course, reverse again. Yet there are reasons to believe this will not happen in the foreseeable future.

First, a successful restructuring of the economy is likely to take a long time. After seven decades of a bureaucratic command economy, change will be difficult and, for many, painful. Nevertheless, Perestroika appears to have widespread support among the intelligentsia. They see it as absolutely essential if the Soviet Union is to avoid an economic decline that could cause it to become a second- or third-rate power. They also consider it essential to making it possible for the population at large to attain a decent standard of living. On the other hand, many party officials, who see their authority and perquisites being undermined by a greater reliance on market forces, are opposed, as are many bureaucrats, for similar reasons. A number of defense establishment leaders are concerned about the projected decline in force numbers and arms expenditures. The workers, importuned to work harder and drink less, do not yet see the rewards in terms of more and better consumer goods. Thus, Perestroika is bound to be difficult and take an agonizingly long time.[10]

These problems, of course, raise questions about Gorbachev's future. Will the opponents of Perestroika mount a successful drive to replace him and revert to the policies of Brezhnev? One cannot be sure, but at least among the Soviet intelligentsia there is a widespread conviction that reversion to the old system would doom the Soviet Union to a reduced status in the world by the year 2000. In a meeting with U.S. counterparts in New York in October 1988, a number of Soviet scholars declared that, with or without Gorbachev, Perestroika was imperative and had to come. Moreover, they believed it must continue, no matter who the Soviet leader may be.[11]

It would appear, then, that the new Soviet attitude toward the United Nations and the office of the secretary general is likely to continue. What are the implications of this change in the Soviet attitude for the future of the United Nations and the selection of a secretary general? First, the Soviet interest in reduced tensions and the peaceful resolution of disputes offers new opportunities for the United Nations to provide good offices or act as a mediator or face-saver. And, as indicated in the Gorbachev and Petrovsky statements, this kind of activity clearly implies the need for an effective secretary general whose leadership and integrity are respected by the parties concerned.

Second, the secretary general cannot succeed unless he can obtain the confidence and cooperation of the parties concerned. When the major powers are in accord, prospects for cease-fires and peaceful settlement are improved but not guaranteed. For at least a year before Iran agreed to a cease-fire, the Soviet Union, the United States, and the other members of the Security Council had declared that the fighting should stop. For the principles of the U.N. charter to govern the behavior of states, governments must be willing to forego the use or threat of force in the pursuit of their national objectives.

Thus, the change in the attitude of the Soviet Union was not by itself responsible for the "epidemic of peace" during the past year. But it did have a significant impact and other governments and the secretary general added the additional ingredients required.

These events suggest the possibility of a rebirth for the United Nations. Are governments prepared to rededicate themselves to

the principles enunciated in the charter in 1945 and so often violated? Can they see that the alternative is international anarchy, a disastrous arms race, continuing large-scale bloodshed and a threatened biosphere? If they can, prudence argues that they cooperate together in a reborn United Nations.

What are the major tasks facing a revitalized United Nations? *First*, there is conflict control and resolution. The United Nations has a most important role to play in helping to resolve regional conflicts, as in Afghanistan, the Iran–Iraq war, Namibia and Central America. Accordingly, as in those instances, the Security Council must emphasize negotiations in private, informal meetings and try to minimize inflammatory public speeches that exacerbate situations. A particular effort must be made to avoid inflammatory polemics by countries that are not parties to the dispute. A display of one-sidedness in disputes by either the Council or the secretary general, except where one side is clearly in violation of the Charter, is bound to make the aggrieved party reluctant to use United Nations mediation or good offices. In order to be effective, the Council and the secretary general must be perceived to be fair and unbiased by all parties to a dispute.

Second, while Soviet–United States cooperation offers welcome new opportunities, the two countries must be careful not to give the impression that they are a condominium dictating to the other members. There is, of course, one built-in brake. Any substantive decision of the Council requires the affirmative votes of nine of the fifteen members; consequently, the superpowers must win the support of some of the small and medium-sized countries that are Council members. Seven of these nonpermanent members are Third World countries; therefore, they have, in effect, a collective veto. Of course, the two "superpowers" must also consult with the other permanent members, France, China, and the United Kingdom, any of which has veto power over Council decisions. Thus, cooperation between the USSR and the United States will not do the job by itself, but it does remove an obstacle that has hampered the United Nations during most of its history: paralysis by the Cold War.

It should be noted that improved Soviet–West relations, while they appear to reduce the threat of war in Europe, have not meant the decline of violence and war in other parts of the world. In

the Soviet Union itself nationalism has reasserted itself in various republics, notably in the Baltic States, Moldavia, and Azerbaijan where clashes between the Armenians and the Azeris have become so violent as to elicit intervention by Soviet troops. Fighting continues in Ethiopia, Myanmar (formerly Burma), Cambodia, and the Sudan, and the potential for violent eruptions and war exists in many other parts of Asia and Africa. Consequently, it is most important to have a vigilant, working Security Council, capable of action and commanding the respect of disputing or warring parties.

Another potential threat is the reported proliferation of nuclear weapons beyond the five countries permitted to have them under the Nuclear Non-Proliferation Treaty endorsed by the U.N. General Assembly in 1968 (G.A. Res. 2373, 12 June 1968). There are at least a dozen "threshold" countries that either have produced nuclear weapons, are close to producing them or have the scientific/industrial capacity to do so. It would be ironic and tragic if new nuclear weapons countries emerge just as the superpowers are cutting their nuclear arsenals drastically. This is a security threat that must be addressed at the United Nations.

Third, the Security Council should give new consideration to the use of coercive force to deal with threats to the peace, breaches of the peace, or acts of aggression. To date military force has been authorized by the Security Council only once, against North Korea in 1950. It was possible then only because the Soviets were boycotting the Council. Participation by member states was voluntary, and sixteen countries provided combat troops.

Given the new Soviet position toward the United Nations, it might be feasible to consider other military actions involving less than the full membership. Article 48 of the United Nations charter states "1. The action required to carry out the decisions of the Security Council for the maintenance of international peace and security shall be taken by all the Members of the United Nations *or by some of them*, as the Security Council may determine" (emphasis added). Thus, if the Security Council determines that there has been a threat to the peace, breach of the peace, or act of aggression (Art. 39), it could authorize one member or a number of members to take such action. A permanent member could vote for the operation or abstain, if it had no objection to the operation

but did not want to participate. For example, if a threat to peace arose in Rumania, the United States might vote for or abstain on a resolution authorizing a Soviet action. (If the United States objects, it could, of course, use its veto.) Such *authorized* use of force would expose even more starkly any use of force in violation of the Charter or other international law.

On a number of occasions permanent members have acquiesced in *peacekeeping* operations which they would not vote for or pay for; for example, UNEF I, Cyprus. Why not enforcement action by one or more members authorized by the Security Council? Even the prospect of such action might make Security Council warnings more forceful and credible.

Fourth, there should be increased emphasis on timely preventive action with respect to disputes and situations which may threaten international peace and security. Such action is foreseen in a Declaration approved by the General Assembly on 5 December 1988 in its Resolution 43/51 (Declaration on the Prevention and Removal of Disputes and Situations Which May Threaten International Peace and Security and on the Role of the United Nations in this Field). This Declaration calls first of all for states to act in a manner that will not give rise to such disputes and situations and to endeavor to resolve their disputes through bilateral or regional negotiations. Other important provisions are:

5. States concerned should consider approaching the relevant organs of the United Nations in order to obtain advice or recommendations on preventive means for dealing with a dispute or situation;

6. Any State party to a dispute or directly concerned with a situation, particularly if it intends to request a meeting of the Security Council, should approach the Council, directly or indirectly, at an early stage and, if appropriate, on a confidential basis;

7. The Security Council should consider holding from time to time meetings, including at a high level with the participation, in particular, of Ministers for Foreign Affairs, or consultations to review the international situation and search for effective ways of improving it;

8. In the course of the preparation for the prevention or removal of particular disputes or situations, the Security Council should consider making use of the various means at its disposal, including the appointment of the Secretary-General as rapporteur for a specified question;

9. When a particular dispute or situation is brought to the attention of the Security Council without a meeting being requested the Council should consider holding consultations with a view to examining the facts of the dispute or situation and keeping it under review, with the assistance of the Secretary-General when needed; the States concerned should have the opportunity of making their views known;

10. In such consultations, consideration should be given to employing such informal methods as the Security Council deems appropriate, including confidential contacts by its President;

11. In such consultations the Security Council should consider inter alia: (a) Reminding the States concerned to respect their obligations under the Charter; (b) Making an appeal to the States concerned to refrain from any action which might give rise to a dispute or lead to the deterioration of the dispute or situation; and (c) Making an appeal to the States concerned to take action which might help to remove, or to prevent the continuation or deterioration of, the dispute or situation.

12. The Security Council should consider sending, at an early stage, fact-finding or good offices missions or establishing appropriate forms of United Nations presence, including observers and peace-keeping operations, as a means of presenting the further deterioration of the dispute or situation in the areas concerned;

• • • • •

20. The Secretary-General, if approached by a State or States directly concerned with a dispute or situation, should respond swiftly by urging the States to seek a resolution or adjustment by peaceful means of their own

choice under the Charter and by offering his good offices or other means at his disposal, as he deems appropriate;

21. The Secretary-General should consider approaching the states directly concerned with a dispute or situation in an effort to prevent it from becoming a threat to the maintenance of international peace and security;

22. The Secretary-General should, where appropriate, consider making full use of fact-finding capabilities, including, with the consent of the host State, sending a representative or fact-finding missions to areas where a dispute or a situation exists; where necessary, the Secretary-General should also consider making the appropriate arrangements;

23. The Secretary-General should be encouraged to consider using, at as early a stage as he deems appropriate, the right that is accorded to him under Article 99 of the Charter; (Article 99 gives the secretary general the right to "bring to the attention of the Security Council any matter which in his opinion may threaten the maintenance of international peace and security.")

The emphasis in this declaration on cooperation between the Security Council and the secretary general and on the role of the secretary general is noteworthy. It further underlines the importance of the secretary general in this new context of world politics.

The establishment of the Office for Research and the Collection of Information (ORCI) has given the secretary general a new arm of analytical information and early warning. Thus, he is in a better position to fulfill his responsibility under Article 99. The secretary general has used this authority very rarely, but the changed attitudes of members provide an opportunity for him to be more active, particularly in bringing attention to such situations or disputes in an incipient stage before they erupt into conflict.

ORCI is a relatively young institution, still in its early stages of development. It should be enabled to gather a much wider and deeper harvest of information and data. This might include informal

consultations with representatives of well-informed member states; the use of observer satellites, reports from U.N. Development Program (UNDP) and Specialized Agency Representatives in the field; contacts with research institutions and analysis of their products; review and analysis of media reports and the ad hoc dispatch by the secretary general of special representatives and observers. A data base for the U.N. system, projected by the U.N. University, would make a valuable contribution.

A key factor in preventive diplomacy will be the degree of encouragement and cooperation afforded by the members of the United Nations, particularly by the permanent members of the Security Council and other major countries, like Japan, India, Nigeria, Brazil, and Federal Republic of Germany, Canada, and Australia. The information and data they possess could be of enormous help to the secretary general.

While the secretary general and his deputies have done a commendable job of providing good offices and mediation, a significant increase in their work load might strain their capacities. Consequently, it would be helpful to prepare a roster of distinguished individuals who might be called on to report on situations and/or provide good offices, mediation, or arbitration on request or with the consent of the parties. Moreover, greater resort should be made to the judges of the International Court of Justice (ICJ), either as individuals, in panels, or sitting as a Court.

Fifth, the capacity for peacekeeping, a major U.N. success recognized by the Nobel Peace award in 1988, should be strengthened. There are no specific provisions on peacekeeping in the U.N. charter. Various scholars have cited chapter VI, arguing that peacekeeping is ancillary to the pacific settlement of disputes. Others cite Article 40, chapter VII, which addresses "provisional measures." Also, a General Assembly committee has attempted for more than two decades to develop agreed guidelines without success.

At this point it would appear to be more fruitful to focus on practical measures to improve the functioning and financing of peacekeeping operations rather than pursue attempts to amend the Charter or establish detailed guidelines. On a "common law" basis, UNEF II, UNDOF, and the operations in the Persian gulf

and Namibia have established precedents and modus vivendi for future operations. There are, however, serious problems with financing, putting an unjust burden on countries that provide contingents and are not adequately compensated because of a shortfall of funds. Improvements are also needed in the training of troops for peacekeeping. It would, therefore, be useful to have a roster of contingents that member states would be willing to provide and to work out cooperative training procedures. Also, some operations which have been going on for many years (UNFICYP, UNDOF) have stemmed the violence but show no sign of ending. Ways should be sought to have peacemaking linked to peacekeeping operations at the outset and to keep pressure on the parties to settle their disputes.

Sixth, as the two superpowers agree on mutual arms reductions, the United Nations should direct its attention to negotiating agreements or conventions that will reduce the arms burden of developing countries and lessen the danger from chemical weapons and the proliferation of nuclear weapons. The superpowers, by setting an example, are in a better position to urge arms restraints and reductions on others.

Seventh, there is an opportunity for a new approach at the U.N. toward economic development. The recent trend toward more pragmatic, less confrontational consideration of North–South economic issues should be encouraged and should be aimed at practical results. The all-or-nothing approach embodied in "global negotiations" for a New International Economic Order (NIEO), characteristic of the 1970s and much of the 1980s, tended to produce nothing but a North–South standoff. Except for certain "new tigers" in East Asia which have developed rapidly, most of the Third World countries have experienced either negligible or negative growth over the past decade, and many carry a very enormous debt burden.

Yet there is some cause for hope that the 1990s may see an acceleration of economic growth among Third World countries. One factor is the more pragmatic approach taken in the last two years. Another is that such growth is already a reality in an increasing number of countries of East Asia. The growth virus, having infected Japan, Korea, Taiwan, Hong Kong, and Singapore, is now invading Malaysia, Thailand, Indonesia, and even Vietnam. There

is every reason to suppose that the contagion will encompass other countries, particularly if the industrialized countries help to spread it.

The task is, therefore, to study the breakthrough in economic growth that is occurring in East Asia and to consider how it might be replicated elsewhere: that is, in Southern Asia, Africa, and Latin America. The following are offered as possible approaches that might be pursued:

- To what extent and how should present strategies for Third World development be adapted in the light of what has been happening in East Asia, and to take into account changing attitudes towards the role of market forces and private entrepreneurship?

- How can the debt crisis be resolved?

- What trade concessions to developing countries would best promote their economic growth?

- How can the role of transnational corporations, which already play an important part in the industrialization of many developing countries, be expanded further on terms that will be mutually beneficial and will not impinge on the sovereign rights of the host country?

- Can the institutional machinery of the U.N. system be rationalized in the changing environment where North–South relations are becoming less confrontational? Specifically, should there be rival institutions in the same field; such as the U.N. Conference on Trade and Development (UNCTAD) favored by the developing countries, and the General Agreement on Tariffs and Trade (GATT), favored by the industrialized nations?

- Should there be a new intergovernmental policy-making authority to provide consensus-type guidance to the agencies of the U.N. system? The U.N. Economic and Social Council (ECOSOC) which has had theoretical responsibility for such policy guidance, has long been moribund and has grown to an unwieldly size. Perhaps a new Ministerial Board, as suggested by the U.N. Association of the USA, might succeed where ECOSOC has failed.[12]

There is, further, the problem of the least developed countries, which continue to need capital (as grants or soft loans) and technical assistance to develop the infrastructure required to provide a sound basis for public and private investments, both internal and external. On the one hand, there are now more potential donors, as more countries have become prosperous. On the other, the dramatic changes in Eastern Europe and the Soviet Union, with shifts toward market economies, have induced the pledge of large amounts of aid and private investment to those areas, in competition with the needs of developing countries and especially the poorest ones. This is a situation which cries out for enlightened consideration at the United Nations, the World Bank, and the International Monetary Fund (IMF).

Eighth, there are new opportunities for progress in the area of human rights. Not long ago U.N. organs focused their attention almost exclusively on violations in South Africa, Israel, and Chile, while ignoring egregious violations elsewhere. Now there are rapporteurs investigating situations in Cuba, Iran, Iraq, Afghanistan, El Salvador, Kampuchea, Romania, and Albania. Glasnost (openness) in the Soviet Union and revolutionary changes in Eastern Europe have given a new reality to human rights discussion—one of the fruits of the Helenski Conference on Security and Cooperation in Europe. The greater willingness of the Soviets and Eastern Europeans to have an open discussion of human rights issues should pave the way for a less biased, consequently more effective, approach at the United Nations.

Ninth, there is room for improvement in U.N. programs for refugees and disaster relief. As indicated above, the U.N. record was creditable even in the Waldheim era. But the magnitude of the problems, particularly in Africa, Asia, and Central America, is growing; refugees now number more than 17 million. The plight of the Vietnamese threatened with repatriation from Hong Kong has commanded media attention lately, but it is only the tip of the iceberg. A new, concerted international effort is certainly warranted.

As for disaster management, cogent suggestions for improvement have been put forward by Prince Sadruddin Aga Khan, former high commissioner for refugees (1965-1977) and currently coordinator of the United Nations' Humanitarian and Economic

Assistance relating to Afghanistan. In essence he proposes that the information and communications capacity of the U.N. Disaster Relief Organization (UNDRO) be rapidly improved so that it may serve as a clearinghouse of information on the technical services, training courses, and other prevention measures that are necessary, planned, or already under way around the world. ''Moreover, there should be a much clearer line of authority from the field through the UNDRO (U.N. Disaster Relief Organization) Coordinator to the Secretary General and a more effective media strategy.''[13]

Tenth, there is the drug traffic problem, a growing worldwide threat and of great concern to the United States. Addressing a special session of the U.N. General Assembly on 20 February 1990, Secretary of State James A. Baker called for the adoption of a global program against trade in illegal narcotics. Such trade is estimated to be worth $500 billion a year, more than the oil trade and second only to trade in arms. Representatives of developing countries where production, processing, and transfer take place acknowledge their part of the problem but argue that reducing consumption is at least as important. Moreover, they call for economic aid from the industrialized countries so that they provide the help their farmers need to stop growing drug crops.[14] Despite these significant differences, all sides agreed on the gravity of the problem and the urgent need for the United Nations to address it.

The United Nations has been concerned with the drug problem throughout its existence. In February 1946 its Economic and Social Council established a Commission on Narcotic Drugs. The Commission reviews the global drug situation and assists the Council on monitoring the implementation of international conventions and in the preparation of new instruments to strengthen international drug control. These included the Single Convention on Narcotic Drugs (1961), the Convention on Psychotropic Substances (1971), and the United Nations Convention Against Illicit Traffic in Narcotic Drugs and Psychotropic Substances (1988). These instruments, and the work of the Commission and of the U.N. Division of Narcotic Drugs, have been useful in fostering international cooperation to control the drug traffic. But the problem has now exploded to the point where new major national

and international efforts are urgently needed, with the United Nations as a central focal point.

Finally, and most important, is the role of the United Nations in alerting governments to threats to the environment and in providing a forum for communication and cooperation. Prior to the 1972 U.N. Conference on the Environment convened in Stockholm on the initiative of Sweden, few governments took the problem seriously enough to establish cabinet posts. Since then every major or medium-sized country has established a ministerial level post or agency concerned with the environment (in the United States, the Environmental Protection Agency). Now there is widespread concern over serious threats to the biosphere, notably the danger of atmospheric warming as levels of carbon dioxide and other gases rise. Farming and many other economic activities could be affected very seriously and extensive coastal areas inundated as glaciers melt. Acid rain and pollution of streams, rivers, seas, and lakes are already commonplace. The Chernobyl disaster, in which winds carried radioactive particles to the countries of Central and Western Europe, underlined another serious threat to the environment. These problems do not respect national boundaries; hence, international cooperation is essential, and the United Nations has a key role to play in alerting governments to global problems and fostering cooperation to deal with them. Indeed, the environmental challenge will be one of the key problems facing the world and the United Nations in the 1990s.

These eleven areas of activity constitute a formidable agenda and are a manifestation of growing interdependence. The vast changes that have taken place in the world since 1945 will require a major effort of imagination and reorganization in the U.N. system. As Brian Urquhart observes: "The problem is to convert an intergovernmental system in which national sovereignty and interests are paramount, to an international system in which an increasing number of activities beyond the control of individual governments can be carried out by international, or even supranational institutions. The particular interests involved and the extreme sensitivity of governments in matters touching on their sovereignty will inevitably make this evolution laborious and frustrating."[15]

It is clear that such an evolution, along with the challenges already facing the United Nations in the maintenance of peace, will depend on the willingness of governments, particularly the Soviet Union and the United States. We have already noted the 180 degree change in the Soviet position, toward strong support for an effective United Nations. The United States, initially one of the strongest supporters, went through a period of disenchantment in the 1970s and early 1980s as the Third World nations, constituting a majority, dominated the General Assembly. The Assembly adopted many resolutions that Americans considered grossly unfair, particularly with regard to the Arab–Israeli dispute and economic issues. The most devastating in its impact on the attitude of Americans toward the U.N. was the resolution equating Zionism with racism, which we have discussed in chapter 3.

But recent statements by Presidents Reagan and Bush suggest that the United States is once again looking toward the United Nations as a useful vehicle for certain important aspects of American foreign policy. In his last address to the General Assembly, Reagan replaced his earlier anti-U.N. rhetoric with a more hopeful view of the organization. Referring to the restructuring that had been instituted in response to demands by the United States and other industrialized countries, he said, "Precisely because of these changes, today the United Nations has the opportunity to live and breathe and work as never before. . . . We are determined that the United Nations should succeed and serve the cause of peace of humankind."[16] In keeping with this statement, Reagan asked Congress to take action which would enable the United States to start paying its arrears in U.N. assessments.

President Bush has also expressed a positive attitude. In a letter to the new chairman of the U.N. Association of the USA, John C. Whitehead, he wrote: "You can be sure that my Administration will do its best to strengthen the U.N. and to reassert positive leadership there."[17] Whitehead's acceptance of the post of chairman of the Association is in itself a good augery. He served as deputy secretary of state in the Reagan Administration, knows Bush and other key figures on Bush's team well, and is highly respected by them.

Bush has also asked Congress to appropriate funds to pay off U.S. arrears of U.N. assessments, which had grown by January

1990 to approximately $430 million. (The next largest delinquent is South Africa [$37 million] which has been denied participation in the U.N. General Assembly since 1975, followed by Iran, which owes $12 million.)[18] The American failure to pay these assessments has caused a serious financial crisis at the United Nations. It casts a shadow over the future of the organization. It remains to be seen whether the president is ready to exert his influence with a reluctant Congress to pay what the United States owes.

With Soviet and American support and a new spirit among states members of the United Nations, the organization should be in a good position to deal with the challenging agenda of the 1990s. These challenges make the role of the secretary general to be elected in 1991 crucially important. The world has been fortunate in having Javier Perez de Cuellar in that office. He is a man of recognized integrity, great patience, and courage who is highly respected by the member governments. But his election was, to a significant degree, a matter of chance, the same process that has resulted in the election of secretaries general of varying quality. Moreover, he is now over seventy and, having served ten years in an exhausting job, may not be interested in a third five-year term. Given the challenges ahead in the 1990s, it is essential to use a process that will ensure candidates of the highest quality and screening that will avoid the possibility of another Waldheim. In the past there has been no search worthy of the name. Candidates simply put themselves forward or were promoted by particular delegations. Then, after campaigning by the candidates and informal discussions among members of the Security Council, a candidate emerged who could avoid the veto of a permanent member. The post is much too important to be left to such casual procedures.

No self-respecting universities or corporations would choose a leader that way. They carry out extensive searches, check backgrounds carefully and will sometimes woo a person who has not even been a candidate for the job.

One way to improve the process would be for the Security Council to set up, at least nine months before a secretary general is to be appointed, a special committee to conduct a search and examine the records of all those who might be considered by the

Council. Such a search committee would have looked into backgrounds in 1971 and might have raised questions about a former Wehrmacht officer like Waldheim. Foreign ministers and the secretary of state do not have time for such investigations, nor do the busy permanent representatives at the United Nations. *Members of the Secretariat, who screen applicants for other positions, have no role in the choice of their chief.* Thus a vacuum is left in searching for and screening potential secretaries general, a vacuum which could be filled by a search committee. The goal would be to recommend people who have high potentials for leadership, administration, and diplomacy. The number to be recommended to the Council might be from three to five. Each of them should have a day-long interview at a closed meeting of the search committee, during which their backgrounds and qualifications should be examined in detail. This procedure would offer the additional advantage of giving the ten nonpermanent members a genuine role in the selection of the secretary general instead of merely ratifying the candidate who has avoided the veto of one of the five permanent members.

Would such a procedure eliminate politics? Certainly not. That is neither possible nor desirable. Members of the search committee would, after all, be designated by the fifteen government members of the Security Council. But the search committee, whose members would concentrate on the selection process for many months, would provide a system for seeking excellence within the parameters of political reality. Thus the Council would be provided a choice among the best qualified rather than "the least undesirable."

This same principle, although not the procedure, should then be applied to the Secretariat. As we noted in chapter 3, it has strayed from the concept of a truly international civil service. A secretary general chosen by search and not beholden to any particular government would have the independence to resist political pressures in filling Secretariat jobs. It has been suggested that the secretary general be limited to one term; thus, he would not be tempted to hand out jobs in order to help his reelection.[19]

Waldheim himself suggested the following measures as a way to utilize the secretary general more fully:

The Secretary General needs more authority to co-ordinate the activities of the many loosely articulated parts of the United Nations system. He should be given specific authority to cut through procedural complexities by convening high-level meetings to defuse threatening international problems through negotiation.

He should be invited to chair multilateral conferences when it is important to prevent procedural obstructionism and facilitate agreement. His authority over the staff of the Secretariat should be strengthened against encroachment by patronage-hungry groups of members.

As a counterpart to his authority to propose items for consideration by United Nations organs, he should likewise receive authority to propose clearing the agenda of those organs of subjects that are endlessly debated year after year with no prospect of progress. Where it would help to facilitate compromise, he should be permitted to introduce resolutions in United Nations organs in his own name.[20]

These are useful suggestions, but they do not get to the heart of the matter; that is, the confidence of member governments in the integrity, leadership qualities, administrative skills, and diplomatic ability of the secretary general. There is no way to legislate greater authority for the secretary general over the Specialized Agencies, which are under the authority of their own intergovernmental bodies. They can be induced to cooperate and coordinate activities by a secretary general they respect; they cannot be coerced. Similarly, a secretary general will be invited to chair multilateral conferences if the parties consider his chairmanship useful. While it might be helpful at times to have the secretary general authorized to introduce resolutions in his own name, any good ideas can be discussed with delegates who can put them forward as resolutions. Alternatively, they may be included in the secretary general's Annual Report, where they will be picked up by interested delegates. As for strengthening his authority over the staff ''against encroachment by patronage-hungry groups of members,'' that will depend on the attitude of governments and the backbone and integrity of the secretary general. Waldheim himself showed little backbone in resisting

pressures. On the contrary, his predilection for intervening in the appointment and promotion of Secretariat staff, often for political reasons, made the situation worse.

The real issue is not changes in formal procedures that might facilitate the tasks of the secretary general. It is, rather, the willingness of governments to use the United Nations to deal with major issues of peace and security and to endow the secretary general with the necessary trust and scope.

The nations of the world are again at a crossroads, as they were in 1945 and 1971. Down one road lies a floundering United Nations, peripheral to major international issues, and an anarchic international system. The other road could lead to a reborn United Nations, in which the nations cooperate to maintain international peace and security, defend the viability of the biosphere, protect human rights, and advance economic and social development.

The year of 1988 may well prove to have been the turning point. It was when the United Nations, and particularly the secretary general, helped to stop the fighting between Iran and Iraq and to bring about the withdrawal of Soviet forces from Afghanistan. It was the year when progress was made, with U.N. assistance, toward independence for Namibia; the withdrawal of South African and Cuban forces from Angola; movement toward the peaceful settlement of the Morocco–Polisario dispute in the Western Sahara; and toward the withdrawal of Vietnamese forces from Cambodia. It was the year that U.N. peacekeeping forces were awarded the Nobel Peace Prize. And it was the year when the Soviet Union, which had for decades opposed the principle of U.N. peacekeeping forces and advocated a passive role for the secretary general, not only reaffirmed a dramatic reversal on both counts but also proposed a more active role for the United Nations in the service of comprehensive international peace and security.

These developments could provide a new opportunity for governments to build together an effective, revitalized United Nations. Will they demonstrate that they take serious the pledges they made in accepting the charter? Will there be a sustained, cooperative endeavor to make the United Nations work in the way it was intended? The answer is of vital importance to the well-being and survival of humanity.

As for the United States, the late Arthur J. Goldberg pointed the way:

> It is our determination to rely on the United Nations, to use the United Nations, to have confidence in the United Nations' operating capacity. The stakes are so high that we should be willing to take chances on the United Nations' capacity to act, and to back it up even when some of its particular decisions go against our immediate national desires. For the risks of a United Nations without the capacity to act are far greater than the risks of a United Nations with that capacity.[21]

One major indicator will be the way the United States and other governments approach the election of a new secretary general in 1991. This will provide a rare opportunity to demonstrate that the U.N.'s successes of 1988–1989 were not a flash in the pan and that the members are determined to put the United Nations back on the road that its charter envisaged. If they are, they will take very seriously the choice of a man to lead the organization. They will pick a leader of recognized stature, integrity, and ability, whom they can and will trust to deal with major issues of peace, security, and human survival. They will select a captain who will take account of the political winds and navigate skillfully toward humanity's urgent goals, not one who will bend with every wind as a means toward personal advancement.

Thus we shall witness a fateful choice. Why not the best?

Notes

Chapter 1

1. Brian Urquhart, *A Life in Peace and War* (New York: Harper and Row, 1987), 227–30.

2. World Jewish Congress Commission on the Holocaust and Crimes of the Nazis, *Waldheim's Nazi Past: The Dossier*, (New York: World Jewish Congress, 1988). See also, Robert Edwin Herzstein, *Waldheim: The Missing Years* (New York: Morrow, 1988).

3. Herzstein, *Waldheim*; Bernard Cohen and Luc Rosenzweig, *Le Mystère Waldheim* (Paris: Guillemard, 1986).

4. Kurt Waldheim, "Survivor Course" in *In the Eye of the Storm* (Bethesda, Md.: Adler and Adler, 1986), chapter 2.

5. Interview with Lieselotte Waldheim, 1 May 1989, Geneva, Switzerland.

6. World Jewish Congress, *Waldheim's Nazi Past*, 43–44.

7. Waldheim, *In the Eye of the Storm*, 17.

8. Herzstein, *Waldheim*, 121.

9. International Commission of Historians, Report in *Profil* no. 7 (Vienna: 15 February 1988), 1–48.

10. Interview with Professor Yehuda Wallach, 8 August 1989, Tel Aviv.

11. Interview with Kurt Waldheim, 8 August 1988, Salzburg, Austria.

12. *Encounter*, vol. 81, no. 3, (Sept/Oct 1988): 27–31.

13. Herzstein, *Waldheim*, 259–60.

14. Kurt Waldheim, *Kurt Waldheim's Wartime Years: A Documentation* (Vienna, Austria: Carl Gerold's Sohn, 1987), 131–32.
15. Ibid., 133.
16. Herzstein, *Waldheim*, 208–9.
17. Christopher Simpson, *Blowback: America's Recruitment of Nazis and Its Effects on the Cold War*, (New York: Weidenfeld and Nicolson, 1988).
18. Herzstein, *Waldheim*, 257.
19. Herzstein, *Waldheim*, 257–58.
20. See "Among Those Interviewed," below.

Among Those Interviewed

George Davidson (Canada), Undersecretary General for Administration and Management, 1973-1981

Ambassador Ismat Kittani (Iraq), Chef de Cabinet to Waldheim, 1971-1974

Ambassador Fereydoun Hoveyda (Iran), former Permanent Representative to the United Nations, 1974-1981

Rafeeudin Ahmed (Pakistan), former Chef de Cabinet to Waldheim

Herbert Reis, former Legal Counselor, U.S. Mission to the United Nations

Michael Berlin, U.N. correspondent, *New York Post* and *Washington Post*

Arkady Shevchenko, Undersecretary General for Political and Security Affairs, 1973-1977

Ambassador Gerald Helman, former Director of U.N. Political Affairs, Department of State

Neil Sher, Director, Office of Special Investigations, U.S. Department of Justice

Jean-Francois Giuliani, Spokesman for the secretary general

Ambassador David Popper, Former Assistant Secretary of State for International Organization Affairs, Department of State. Prepared first draft of Waldheim's Book, *In the Eye of the Storm.*

Robert Rosenstock, Legal Counselor, U.S. Mission to the United Nations

Doctor Nathan Pelcovits, School of Advanced International Studies, Johns Hopkins University

Samuel De Palma, Former Assistant Secretary of State for International Organization Affairs

Robert Schiffer, Former speech writer for Waldheim

Elan Steinberg, World Jewish Congress

Doctor Richard F. Pedersen, Counselor of the Department of State, 1969-1973

Doctor Joseph J. Sisco, former Undersecretary of State for Political Affairs

Professor Oscar Schachter, School of Law, Columbia University

Peggy Sanford Carlin, Vice President, U.N. Association of the USA

Sir Brian Urquhart, Undersecretary General for Special Political Affairs, 1973-1985

C. V. Narasimhan, Chef de Cabinet to Waldheim, 1971-1972

Eugeniusz Wyzner (Poland), Undersecretary General, United Nations

Hans Janitshek (Australia), Journalist, Former Secretary General, Socialist International 1969-1976, Special Assistant to Waldheim 1976-1979

James Jonah (Sierra Leone), Assistant Secretary General, United Nations

Richard C. Hottelet, former U.N. Correspondent, CBS News

James Sutterlin (United States), former Director, Representation Unit, Executive Office of the secretary general

Maurice Strong, (Canada) former Executive Director, United Nations Environment Program

Joseph Tekoah, former Permanent Representative of Israel to the United Nations

Gideon Rafael, former Permanent Representative of Israel to the United Nations

William P. Rogers, Secretary of State, 1969-1973

George Saddler, former Counselor, U.S. Mission to the United Nations

Avi Beker, Executive Director, Israeli Section, World Jewish Congress. Member of Israeli Mission to the United Nations while Waldheim was secretary general

Ambassador William J. Vanden Heuvel, Deputy Permanent Representative of the United States to the United Nations 1979-1981

Ambassador Sverker Astrom, Former Permanent Representative of Sweden to the United Nations

Professor Yehuda Wallach, Member of the International Commission of Historians invited by the Austrian Government to investigate Waldheim's wartime record

Chapter 2

1. Seymour Maxwell Finger, *Your Man at the UN* (New York: New York University Press, 1980), 57–58. Lawrence Weiler and Anne Simons, *The United States and the United Nations: The Search for International Peace and Security* (New York: Carnegie Endowment, 1967), 108.

2. Brian Urquhart, *Hammarskjöld* (New York: Alfred A. Knopf, 1972), 88–94, 131, 505–6. See also, Alexander De Conde, *A History of American Foreign Policy*, 3rd ed. vol. II, (New York: Scribners, 1978), 355 and Ernest W. Lefever, *Crisis in Congo* (Washington, D.C.: Brookings Institution 1965).

3. Conor Cruise O'Brien, *To Katanga and Back* (New York: Simon and Schuster, 1962), 219–88.

4. U.S. Mission to the United Nations (USUN) telegrams to State Department 25 January, 21 February, 11 May, 8 June, 4 August, 29 September, 22 November, 26 November, and 30 November. State Department telegrams to USUN 9 July and 22 September.

5. Max Jakobson, *38. Kerros* (38th Floor) (Helsinki, Otava, 1983), 352–53. (In Finnish)

6. Note on the procedure for appointing the secretary general in the Security Council 15 December 1971, provided by the Secretariat to all Council members.

7. USUN telegram 5116, 17 December 1971.

8. USUN telegram 5135, 17 December 1971.

9. USUN telegram 5149, 18 December 1971.

10. USUN telegram 5157, 20 December 1971.

11. State Dept. telegram to USUN dated 20 December 1971.

12. USUN telegram 5191, 22 December 1971.

13. Note dated 23 December 1971, from USUN to the Austrian Mission to the United Nations.

14. Kurt Waldheim, *In the Eye of the Storm* (Bethesda, Md.: Adler and Adler, 1986), 37.

15. Jakobson, *38. Kerros*, 340.

16. Interview with William Rogers, 7 June 1988.

17. Interview with Joseph Sisco, 11 April 1988, and Richard Pedersen, 4 April 1988.

18. Memorandum of conversation filed by Ben F. Dixon, USUN, 21 January 1971.

19. Memorandum from Robert Rosenstock, counsellor, USUN, to Michael Newlin, chief of political section, USUN, 21 December 1971.

20. Interview with Arkady Shevchenko, former personal aide to Gromyko, 29 March 1988, Washington, D.C.

21. Jakobson, *38. Kerros*, 335–36.

22. Finger, *Your Man*, 197.

23. Interview with William Rogers, 7 June 1988.

24. Jakobson, *38. Kerros*, 347.

25. Waldheim, *In the Eye of the Storm*, 30.

26. GA Res 590 (VI), 2 February 1952, and new Staff Rules, SGB/94, December 1952.

27. U.N. Document St/SGB. Staff Regulations/Rev. 20, 24 February 1949.

28. Interview with Ambassador Ovadia Soffer, 17 July 1988, Israeli Embassy, Paris.

29. U.N. Press release SG/SM3864, 2 May 1986 and General Assembly document A/41/1343, 16 May 1986.

30. Interview with Benjamin Netanyahu, deputy foreign minister of Israel, 8 August 1989, Jerusalem.

31. Interview with Kurt Waldheim, 11 August 1988, Salzburg, Austria.

32. Christopher Simpson, *Blowback: America's Recruitment of the Nazis and Its Effects on the Cold War* (New York: Weidenfeld and Nicolson, 1988).

Chapter 3

1. Mikhail Gorbachev, *Realities and Guarantees for a Secure World* (Moscow: Novesti Publishing House, 1987).

2. General Assembly Official Records (GAOR) (XII), Plenary meeting 26 September 1957, 175.

3. U.N. Press Release, SG/SM 1304 21 May 1965, 3.

4. Thomas Franck, *Nation Against Nation* (New York: Oxford University Press, 1985), 114. Chapter 8 of Franck's book deals very effectively with the "Black Box Function."

5. Brian Urquhart, *A Life in Peace and War* (New York: Harper and Row, 1987), 228–29.

6. Ibid., 230.

7. Seymour Maxwell Finger, "The Maintenance of Peace," in *The Changing United Nations: Options for the United States*, ed. David A. Kay, Proceedings of the Academy of Political Science, vol. 32, no. 4 (1977): 200–204.

8. Urquhart, *A Life*, 229.

9. See for example, the statement by Ambassador Paul J. F. Lusaka (Zambia), president of the 39th Session of the General Assembly, GAOR 18 September 1984.

10. Statement to the General Assembly by Eduard A. Shevardnadze, Soviet foreign minister, unofficial translation by USSR Mission to the United Nations 27 September 1988, 5. See also, the statement by Vladimir Petrovsky, deputy foreign minister, at a press conference in Moscow 19 May 1988 and E. C. Luck and T. T. Gati, "Gorbachev, the United Nations, and U.S. Policy," *The Washington Quarterly*, Autumn 1988, 23.

11. Seymour Maxwell Finger, *American Ambassadors at the UN* (New York: Holmes and Meier, 1987), 322–26.

12. Ibid., 240–41.

13. Interview with Fereydoun Hoveyda, 16 March 1988.

14. Kurt Waldheim, *In the Eye of the Storm* (Bethesda, Md.: Adler and Adler, 1986), 193–94.

15. Seymour Maxwell Finger, "The Effect of the Institutionalization of Anti-Zionism on the Integrity of the United Nations Secretariat", in *Israel Yearbook on Human Rights* vol. 17 (Norwell, Ma.: Kluwer, 1988), 74–78.

16. Ibid., 80–81.

17. Interview with Eric Rouleau, 17 July 1988, Paris.

18. Quoted in Bernard Cohen and Luc Rosenzweig, *Le Mystère Waldheim* (Paris: Guillemard, 1986), 127.

19. Interview with Ovadia Soffer, 7 July 1988, Paris.

20. Seymour Maxwell Finger, "The United Nations and International Terrorism," *The Jerusalem Journal of International Relations*, vol. 10, no. 1 (1988): 15–18.

21. Waldheim, *In the Eye of the Storm*, 41.

22. Finger, "The United Nations and International Terrorism," 12–43.

Chapter 4

1. Interview with Arkady Shevchenko, 29 March 1988, Washington, D.C.

2. Kurt Waldheim, *In the Eye of the Storm*, (Bethesda, Md.: Adler and Adler, 1986), 249.

3. Interview with Shevchenko, 29 March 1988.

4. Interview with Jean-Francois Giuliani, 17 March 1988.

5. Interview with Richard Pedersen, 4 April 1988.

6. Interview with William P. Rogers, 7 June 1988. See also Elaine Sciolino, "Waldheim's U.N. Tenure Seems to Show No Pattern Favoring East or West," *The New York Times*, 14 June 1988, 10; and Michael J. Berlin, "Waldheim passed muster at the U.N. for ten quiet years," *The Sun* (Baltimore), 15 June 1986, A20.

7. Brian Urquhart, *A Life in Peace and War* (New York: Harper and Row, 1987), 265.

8. Thomas M. Franck, *Nation Against Nation* (New York: Oxford University Press, 1985), 171.

9. Urquhart, *A Life*, 240.

10. Ibid., 240.

11. Waldheim, *In the Eye*, 76–77.

12. Ibid., 84–85; see also, Urquhart, *A Life*, 256–57.

13. Letter dated 25 November 1979 from the secretary general addressed to the president of the Security Council.

14. Urquhart, *A Life*, 322–25; see also, Waldheim, *In the Eye*, 5. The fact that the United States was prodding Waldheim to go to Iran was confirmed to us by William Vandenheuvel, in an interview, 18 November 1988, New York. Ambassador Vandenheuvel, as deputy permanent representative, had himself made several approaches urging such a mission by the secretary general.

15. Ibid., 324. See also the statement by the spokesman for the secretary general, 21 January 1981, which includes the text of a letter from Carter to Waldheim expressing gratitude for his efforts on behalf of the hostages.

16. Interview with Donald McHenry, 11 December 1988, Washington, D.C.

17. Urquhart, *A Life*, 226–30.

18. Interview with Kurt Waldheim, 11 August 1988, Salzburg, Austria.

19. Kurt Waldheim, ''Into the Future'' in *The Challenge of Peace* (New York: Rawson Wade, 1980), chapter 10.

20. Waldheim, *In the Eye of the Storm*, 114. For a fuller description of Waldheim's views on the economic goals of the Third World, see Waldheim, *The Challenge of Peace*, ch. 10. The difference in emphasis on the New International Economic Order in the two books appears to reflect the decline in relevance of the NIEO.

21. Franck, *Nation*, 159.

22. Waldheim, *In the Eye of the Storm*, 150; see also Urquhart, *A Life*, 230–32.

23. Ibid., 151.

24. Ibid., 153–54.

25. Quoted in Franck, *Nation*, 151.

26. Ibid., 122.

27. Shirley Hazzard, ''Reflections: The United Nations and Waldheim, Part II,'' *The New Yorker*, 2 October 1989, 75–76.

28. Waldheim, *In the Eye of the Storm*, 146.

Chapter 5

1. Robert Rhodes James, *Staffing the United Nations Secretariat* (Sussex, England: Institute for the Study of International Organizations, monograph, 1970); *Report of the Joint Inspection Unit on Personnel Problems in the United Nations* A/8454 (New York: United Nations, 1971); *Report of the Special Committee for the Review of the United Nations System* A/8728 (New York: United Nations, 1972); Seymour Maxwell Finger and J. F. Mugno, "The Politics of Staffing the United Nations Secretariat," *Orbis*, Spring 1975, 117–45; and Theodor Meron, *The United Nations Secretariat: Rules and Practice* (Lexington, Ma.: Lexington Books, 1977).

2. George Davidson, Statement re Recruitment of Soviet and Other Eastern European nationals for employment in the United Nations Secretariat (1972–1981), 5.

3. Elaine Sciolino, "The U.N.'s Complicated Brand of Office Politics," *The New York Times*, 31 March 1987, D18. She quotes a CIA report stating that one-fourth of the Soviet employees of the Secretariat are intelligence officers who use their assignments "to collect information on U.N. activities; operations; and to collect scientific and technical information of value to the U.S.S.R." (From time to time the FBI catches such a Soviet spy.) The CIA report also states that the Soviet Union nets an estimated $20 million in hard currency from the Secretariat paychecks turned over to the Soviet mission, which then doles out Soviet-level salaries. See also Arkady Shevchenko, *Breaking With Moscow* (New York: Alfred A. Knopf, 1985).

4. Kurt Waldheim, *In the Eye of the Storm* (Bethesda, Md.: Adler and Adler, 1986), 49.

5. Shevchenko, *Breaking with Moscow*, 330–31.

6. Interviews with many Secretariat members or persons who dealt with them, including Richard C. Hottelet, who reported on the United Nations for CBS for more than two decades and had extensive Secretariat contacts, 16 September 1988; George Saddler, currently counsellor at the U.S. Mission to the United Nations, but a Secretariat official under Waldheim 7 January 1989; C. V. Narasimhan, Chef de Cabinet during Waldheim's first twenty-one months as secretariat general; and James Sutterlin, who served in the Executive Office of the secretary general under Waldheim 3 June 1988. Sutterlin relates how Waldheim, meeting with his inner circle of Austrians in the evening, would let fly with nasty remarks about various people. At one point Sutterlin says he felt impelled to mention that he understood German.

7. Quoted in Shirley Hazzard, "Reflections", 86.

8. Ibid., 86–87.

9. Jeane Kirkpatrick, "What Waldheim Didn't Do," Washington Post, 13 April 1986, C7. Having stated that she did not observe any anti-Semitic behavior on Waldheim's part, she adds: "But, in all fairness neither did I notice any effort on his part to intervene in the unfair, unreasonable scapegoating of Israel."

10. Interview with George Saddler, 7 January 1989.

11. Thomas M. Franck, *Nation Against Nation* (New York: Oxford University Press, 1985), 132.

12. Bernard Cohen and Luc Rosenzweig, *Le Mystère Waldheim* (Paris: Guillemard, 1986) 134–37. See also, conversations with former Secretariat official, 22 November 1988.

13. Brian Urquhart, *A Life in Peace and War* (New York: Harper and Row, 1987), 229.

Chapter 6

1. Kurt Waldheim, *In the Eye of the Storm* (Bethesda, Md.: Adler and Adler, 1986) 233.

2. Letter dated 26 November 1980 from Congressman Solarz to Waldheim and Waldheim's reply dated 19 December 1980; Solarz refers to an article by Martin Peretz in *The New Republic*, 29 September 1980.

3. Waldheim, *In the Eye of the Storm*, 232.

4. Ibid., 235.

5. Ibid., 235.

6. Interview with Ovadia Soffer, Israeli ambassador to France, 17 July 1988.

7. Urquhart, *A Life in Peace and War* (New York: Harper and Row, 1987), 332–33.

8. Mikhail Gorbachev, *Realities and Guarantees for a Secure World* (Moscow: Novosti Publishing House, 1987). See also the statement by Vladimir Petrovsky, Soviet deputy foreign minister, to the U.N. General Assembly, 17 December 1988.

Chapter 7

1. Kurt Waldheim, *In the Eye of the Storm* (Bethesda, Md.: Adler and Adler, 1986), 235.

2. Christopher Simpson, *Blowback: America's Recruitment of Nazis and Its Effect on the Cold War* (New York: Weidenfeld and Nicolson, 1988).

3. Mikhail Gorbachev, *Realities and Guarantees for a Secure World* (Moscow: Novosti Publishing House, 1987), 9.

4. Ibid., 10.

5. Ibid., 15–16.

6. Statement by Vladimir Petrovsky (USSR) to the U.N. General Assembly, (Press release No. 174 by the USSR Mission to the United Nations, 14 October 1988), 4. Also, U.N. Document A/431629, the Soviet proposal for a comprehensive system of international security.

7. Oran R. Young, *The Intermediaries: Third Parties in International Crises* (Princeton: Princeton University Press, 1967), 113–14.

8. Thomas M. Franck, *Nation Against Nation* (New York: Oxford University Press, 1985), 78–82, 15–51.

9. Adlai Stevenson, *Looking Outward* (New York: Harper and Row, 1963), 125–28.

10. For a discussion of the problems of Perestroika, see Anders Asland, *Gorbachev's Struggle for Economic Reform* (Ithaca, N.Y.: Cornell University Press, 1989). See also Bill Keller, "Soviet Economy: A Shattered Dream," *The New York Times*, 13 May 1990, p. 1.

11. Meeting between delegation of the Soviet U.N. Association and the U.N. Association of the USA, 24-26 October 1988, New York. See also David Hollaway, "Gorbachev's New Thinking" and Robert Legvold, "Revolution in Soviet Policy," *Foreign Affairs*, vol. 68 no. 1 (1989): 66–98.

12. Maurice Bertrand, "The Role of the UN in the Economic and Social Fields," in Peter J. Fromuth, ed. *A Successor Vision: The United Nations of Tomorrow* (Lanham, Md.: University Press of America, 1988), 149–60.

13. Prince Sadruddin Aga Khan, "The Role of the U.N. in Disaster Management," in Fromuth, *A Successor Vision*, pp. 165–92.

14. *The New York Times*, 21 February 1990, 3.

15. Brian Urquhart, "The United Nations and its Discontents," in *New York Review of Books*, 15 March 1990, 12.

16. U.N. Document a/42/ 4, 26, September 1988, 22.

17. Letter dated 8 June 1989, from President Bush to John C. Whitehead, chairman of the U.N. Association of the USA.

18. Paul Lewis, "Bush Would Pay Off U.N. Debt over Five Years," *The New York Times*, 3 February 1990, 5. col. 1.

19. Charles William Maynes, "The United Nations in a Divided World," in Book World, *The Washington Post*, 2 March 1986.

20. Waldheim, *In the Eye of the Storm*, 213.

21. Statement by Ambassador Arthur J. Goldberg to the Special Political Committee of the U.N. General Assembly, USUN Press Release 4719, 24 November 1965, 9.

Select Bibliography

Allison, Graham. *Essence of Decision: Explaining the Cuban Missile Crisis.* Boston: Little, Brown and Company, 1971.

Bailey, Sydney D. *The Procedure of the U.N. Security Council.* Oxford: Clarendon Press, 1975.

Berridge, G. R., and A. Jennings, eds. *Diplomacy at the United Nations.* New York: St. Martins Press, 1985.

Bingham, June. *U Thant: The Search for Peace.* New York: Alfred A. Knopf, 1970.

Born, Hans Peter. *Fuer die Richtigkeit: Kurt Waldheim.* Munich: Scheekluth, 1970.

Boudreau, Tom. *Watchman of the Peace: The Prevention Role of the U.N. Secretary-General.* Ph.D. dissertation prepared for Social Science Program, The Maxwell School, Syracuse University, 1985.

Bracken, Paul. *The Command and Control of Nuclear Forces.* New Haven: Yale University Press, 1983.

Chai, F. Y. *Consultations and Consensus in The Security Council.* New York: UNITAR, 1971.

Claude, Inis L., Jr. *Swords into Plowshares: The Problems and Progress of International Organization.* 4th ed. New York: Random House, 1971.

Cohen, Bernard, and Luc Rosenzweig. *Le Mystère Waldheim.* Paris: Guillemard, 1986.

Cuellar, Javier Perez de. *Report of the Secretary-General on the Work of the Organization, 1982.* New York: The United Nations.

De Bono, Edward. *Conflicts: A Better Way to Solve Them.* London: Harrap Limited, 1985.

De Conde, Alexander. *A History of American Foreign Policy.* 3rd ed. vol. II. New York: Scribners, 1978.

Fascell, Dante B., and Gus Yatron. "Congress and the United Nations." *Proteus,* Spring 1988.

Finger, Seymour Maxwell. "The Maintenance of Peace." In *The Changing United Nations,* ed. David A. Kay, Proceedings of the Academy of Political Science, vol. 32, no. 4 (1977): 200–204.

———. *Your Man at the U.N.* New York: New York University Press, 1980.

———. *American Ambassadors at the U.N.* New York: Holmes and Meier, 1987.

———. "The United Nations and International Terrorism", *Jerusalem Journal of International Relations,* vol. 10, no. 1 (1988): 12–43.

———. "The Effect of the Institutionalization of Anti-Zionism on the Integrity of the United Nations Secretariat", *Israel Yearbook on Human Rights,* vol. 17. Norwell, Ma.: Kluwer, 1988, 74–78.

Finger, Seymour Maxwell, and J. F. Mugno. "The Politics of Staffing the United Nations Secretariat," *Orbis* (Spring 1975): 117–45.

Foote, Wilder, ed. *Servant of Peace: A Selection of the Speeches and Statements of Dag Hammarskjöld.* New York: Harper and Row, 1962.

Franck, Thomas M. *Nation Against Nation.* New York: Oxford University Press, 1985.

Goodrich, Leland M., and Eduard Hambro, eds. *Charter of the United Nations: Commentary and Documents.* Boston: World Peace Foundation, 1946.

Gorbachev, Mikhail. *Realities and Guarantees for a Secure World.* Moscow: Novosti Publishing House, 1987.

Gordenker, Leon. *The U.N. Secretary-General and the Maintenance of Peace.* New York: Columbia University Press, 1967.

———. "Development in the U.N. System." In *The U.S., the U.N. and the Management of Global Change,* ed. Toby Trister, New York: New York University Press, 1983.

Gottlieb, Gideon. "The United Nations and Emergency Humanitarian Assistance in India-Pakistan." *The American Journal of International Law,* vol. 66.

Hazzard, Shirley. "Reflections: The United Nations and Waldheim, Part II," *The New Yorker,* 2 October 1989, 74–96.

Herzstein, Robert Edwin. *Waldheim: The Missing Years.* New York: Morrow, 1988.

Holloway, David. "Gorbachev's New Thinking." *Foreign Affairs*, vol. 68, no. 1 (1989) pp. 66–82.

International Commission on Historians. *Report*. In *Profil* (Vienna, Austria), no. 7 (15 Feb. 1988).

Jackson, William D. "The Political Role of the Secretary-General under U Thant and Kurt Waldheim: Development or Decline?" *World Affairs*, 140 (Winter 1978): 230–44.

Jakobson, Max. *38. Kerros* (38th Floor). Helsinki: Otava, 1983 (in Finnish).

Kalb, Madeline G. "The U.N.'s Embattled Peacekeeper." *New York Times Magazine*, 19 Dec. 1982.

Kennedy, Robert F. *Thirteen Days: A Memoir of the Cuban Missile Crisis*. New York: W. W. Norton and Co., 1969.

Lash, Joseph P. *Dag Hammarskjöld*. Garden City, N.Y.: Doubleday and Company, Inc., 1961.

LeBow, Richard Ned. "The Cuban Missile Crisis: Reading the Lessons Correctly." *Political Science Quarterly*, vol. 98, Fall 1983.

Lefever, Ernest. *Crisis in the Congo*. Washington, D.C.: Brookings Institution, 1965.

Legvold, Robert. "Revolution in Soviet Policy." *Foreign Affairs*, vol. 68, no. 1, 1989, 83–98.

Meron, Theodor. *The United Nations Secretariat: Rules and Practice*. Lexington, Ma.: Lexington Books, 1977.

Morgenthau, Hans. *Politics Among Nations*. 4th ed. New York: Alfred A. Knopf, 1967.

Nicol, Davidson, Margaret Croke, and Babatunde Adenivan. *The United Nations Security Council: Towards Greater Effectiveness*. New York: UNITAR, 1982.

O'Brien, Connor Cruise. *To Katanga and Back*. New York: Simon and Schuster, 1962.

———. *The United Nations: A Sacred Drama*. New York: Simon and Schuster, 1968.

Peschota, Vratislav. *The Quiet Approach: A Study of the Good Offices Exercised by the United Nations Secretary-General in the Cause of Peace*. New York: UNITAR, 1972.

Ramcharan, B. G. *Humanitarian Good Offices in International Law: The Good Offices of the United Nations Secretary-General in the Field of Human Rights*. Dordrecht: Martinus Nijhoff Publishers, 1983.

Rhodes James, Robert. *Staffing the United Nations Secretariat*. Sussex, England: Institute for the Study of International Organizations (monograph) 1970.

Roberts, Adam, and Benedict Kingsbury. *United Nations, Divided World*. Oxford: Claredon Press, 1988.

Shevchenko, Arkady. *Breaking With Moscow*. New York: Alfred A. Knopf, 1985.

Schlesinger, Arthur M. *A Thousand Days*. New York: Houghton Mifflin, 1965.

Schwebel, Stephen M. "The Origins and Development of Article 99 of the Charter." *The British Year-Book of International Law*, 1951.

———. *The Secretary-General of the United Nations: His Political Power and Practice*. New York: Greenwood Press, 1962, Harvard.

Simpson, Christopher. *Blowback: America's Recruitment of Nazis and Its Effects on the Cold War*. New York: Weidenfeld and Nicolson, 1988.

Special Committee for the Review of the United Nations System. *Report*. New York: United Nations, 1972 (Document A/8728).

Stevenson, Adlai. *Looking Outward*. New York: Harper and Row, 1963.

UNITAR, *The United Nations and The Maintenance of International Peace and Security*. Dordrecht: Martinus Nijhoff Publishers, 1987.

Urquhart, Brian. *Hammarskjöld*. New York: Alfred A. Knopf, 1972.

———. *A Life in Peace and War*. New York: Harper and Row, 1987.

Waldheim, Kurt. *The Challenge of Peace*. New York: Rawson Wade, 1980.

———. *Building the Future Order*. New York: The Free Press, 1980.

———. *In the Eye of the Storm*. Bethesda, Md.: Adler and Adler, 1986.

———. *Kurt Waldheim's Wartime Years: A Documentation*. Vienna, Austria: Carl Gerold's Son, 1987.

World Jewish Congress Commission on the Holocaust and the Crimes of the Nazis. *Waldheim's Nazi Past: The Dossier*. New York: World Jewish Congress, 1988.

Young, Oran R. *The Intermediaries: Third Parties in International Crises*. Princeton: Princeton University Press, 1967.

Zacher, Mark W. *Dag Hammarskjöld's United Nations*. New York: Columbia University Press, 1970.

———. *International Conflicts and Collective Security*. New York: Praeger, 1979.

Index

About the Authors

SEYMOUR MAXWELL FINGER is a Senior Fellow at the Ralph Bunche Institute on the United Nations at the Graduate Center of the City University of New York. This career diplomat, ambassador, and professor is the author of several books, including *American Ambassadors in the United Nations.*

ARNOLD A. SALTZMAN is Chairman of Vista Resources, Inc., and Honorary Chairman of the National Committee on American Foreign Policy. He has served on various government boards and as ambassador for Presidents Kennedy and Johnson.